Norman Clyde

CLOSE UPS
OF THE
HIGH SIERRA

Jules Eichorn and Hans "Dutch" Leschke on the "Milk Bottle" (14,080'),
the summit block of Starlight Peak, the northwest peak of North Palisade
(Photo by Norman Clyde, Eastern California Museum Collection)

NORMAN CLYDE

CLOSE UPS

OF THE

HIGH SIERRA

Edited & Designed
by Wynne Benti

Spotted Dog Press

CLOSE UPS OF THE HIGH SIERRA

©1997 by Wynne Benti

Published by Spotted Dog Press
Bishop, California

First Edition 1998, Spotted Dog Press

Cover: Temple Crag, Sierra Nevada by Vern Clevenger
Cover inset photograph of Norman Clyde by Cedric Wright,
    The Bancroft Library
Back Cover: Jules Eichorn and Hans "Dutch" Leschke
    on the "Milk Bottle" by Norman Clyde, Eastern California Museum Collection
Original illustrations by Ruth Daly
Book production by Spotted Dog Press

Library of Congress Cataloging-in-Publication Data
Clyde, Norman, 1885-1972.
    Close Ups of the High Sierra/Norman Clyde:
edited by Wynne Benti. — 1st ed.
p.   cm.
    Includes bibliographical references
    ISBN 0-9647530-3-0 (alk. paper)
    1. Mountaineering — Sierra Nevada (Calif. and Nev.) — Guidebooks.
2. Sierra Nevada (Calif. and Nev.) — Guidebooks. 3. Clyde, Norman,
1885 - 1972. I. Benti, Wynne. II Title.
GV199.42.S55C69 1998
796.52'2' 097944 —dc21

                                          97-46658
                                          CIP

Printed in the United States of America

TABLE OF CONTENTS

A note about safety

*Various aspects of mountaineering have certain risks
and hazards associated with them. Some of these hazards include,
but are not limited to, adverse weather conditions, rockfall, exposed
rock, rugged terrain, stream crossings, hypothermia, heat stroke and
heat exhaustion. A book is not a substitute for maps or
mountaineering skill nor can it make climbing or hiking safe for
those who do not practice the principles of safety. Those who are
inexperienced in mountaineering are encouraged to seek training
provided by various mountaineering clubs and
outdoor organizations. There is no substitute for experience,
skill and knowledge of safety procedures.*

ACKNOWLEDGEMENTS

The editor would like to thank the following people for their assistance on this project, beginning with Bonnie Hardwick, Ph.D., Curator of the Bancroft Collection, Western Americana and William M. Roberts, Acting Curator, Pictorial Collections, of the Bancroft Library at the University of California, Berkeley; The Colby Library, Sierra Club, San Francisco; William Michael, Director of the Eastern California Museum in Inyo County; Vern Clevenger; Glen Dawson for his personal insights, and Pete Yamagata for his photography. Mrs. Pat Adler-Ingram whose children climbed with Clyde, hand-transcribed Clyde's entries from his personal journals while he was still alive. And finally, thanks to Edward Zdon and Edmund Benti; Beverly Harry, Inyo County Clerk; Mr. Walter Bolster of Sacramento, and Mr. Thomas H. Jukes.

Walt Wheelock and Andy Zdon relentlessly encouraged me to pursue this project. Both shared a wonderful passion for collecting books, and spent many happy days together in Walt's studio leafing through them and talking about the old days. Sadly, Walt was not here to see this new edition of "Close Ups of the High Sierra." He lived a long, rich life, and when he passed away in November 1997, with him went the end of an era of publishing — when deals were done on a shared word and books sold from the trunk of a car. He was an inspiration to us all.

To Winnie,

Norman

Norman Clyde, circa 1924
(Photo by Perry Evans, *The Sierra Club Albums*, The Bancroft Library)

FOREWORD
by Wynne Benti

A long time ago, in an abandoned ranch house without electricity or plumbing, a man sat at a kitchen table illuminated by the soft flickering light of a kerosene lamp. Driven to the Sierra by his intense love of them, and by a personal tragedy in his past, he hoped to make a few dollars by selling the stories he would write about his climbing trips. With the passage of time, his tales of adventure would preserve an era of western mountaineering history, as told by California's greatest mountaineer.

"Close Ups of the High Sierra" is a journey to the exquisite and remote backcountry of the Sierra Nevada in California, as told by that great mountaineer, Norman Clyde, who was credited with making more first ascents in the Sierra Nevada than Clarence King, John Muir, and William Brewer, combined. In the book *Sierra Nevada*, Weldon Heald said of Clyde, "(he) has probably made more mountain ascents than any other man who ever lived, not excluding Swiss guides. Certainly, he has no rival in the Sierra." Yet in life, Clyde was not a member of any mountaineering aristocracy — his name appeared on no letterheads, nor did he found any great environmental movement or organization.

With a degree in Classic Literature, an old army hat, and great physical endurance, Clyde became a living legend. He drove nails into the soles of his boots for traction, so slick rock, ice and other obstacles could not keep him from reaching the summits of the mountains he wanted to climb. On cold Sierra mornings, he would recite Homer's "Illiad" and "Odyssey" in Greek, while cooking breakfast for climbing partners at the campfire. He was one of a dying breed, a "vanishing Victorian," which was evident in his writing style. One climbing partner remembered him as a proud and sensitive man, who was unable to grasp modern thinking.

Surely, it was a gentler time, before mountaineering became a multi-million dollar industry of aluminum, fluorescent plastic and nylon. Mountaineers were free to climb anywhere in the Sierra Nevada, unregulated by permits and quotas. Many of today's trails had not yet been completed or built. The roads that led from the Owens Valley to the east side of the range were dirt tracks, often hand-dug by the hard work of a miner attempting to scrape out a living from the side of a mountain. Small, quiet towns with names like Lone Pine, Aberdeen and Independence hadn't changed much since first being settled in the mid-1800's by pioneers who journeyed their wagons across the continent to the deepest valley, some 10,000 feet beneath the jagged skyline of the Sierra Nevada to the west, and the White Mountains to the east.

Among the items the young Clyde carried in his large wood-framed pack was a worn leather-bound journal in which he recorded what he saw in the strikingly beautiful yet remote backcountry of the Sierra Nevada — the color of the sky at sunset or dawn; the experience of being caught in a snow storm on a knife-edge ridge at 13,000 feet, or the simple pleasure of walking down a trail in the long shadows of the late afternoon sun.

After losing his last job as a high school principal, Clyde moved into a broken-down ranch house on Baker Creek. It had been abandoned when the Los Angeles Department of Water and Power bought the property for its aqueduct to carry water from the Owens Valley to Los Angeles. It was known that Clyde lived in the house, but he was left alone, without plumbing or electricity to enjoy the visiting field mice, and the kitchen, its rotten wood floor turned to sod. From its window, beyond the tall pines to the stark Sierra crest, his inspiration was the view of Peak 13,920'+, which would one day bear his name. One story became a hundred, on a wide variety of subjects, from how to properly use a wood-axe to fishing for trout along the John Muir Trail. Some stories were sold to the Automobile Club of Southern California for publication in their magazine, "Touring Topics." Most were never published. Instead, he paper-clipped them together and filed them away in cardboard boxes, along with the unopened return envelopes of rejected stories, where they remained for most of the twentieth century.

When "Close Ups of Our High Sierra" was first published by the Auto Club in 1928, it was enthusiastically received. Copies of "Touring Topics" with Clyde's articles quickly disappeared into the libraries of Sierra mountaineers, and soon became collector's items. The original series is reprinted in this new edition as Clyde first wrote them, including the elevations that were then accepted. Also included for the first time, are several of the stories that were never published, but were recently rediscovered, intact with thin yellowed pages and rusted paper clips, just as Clyde left them.

In September of 1997, Walt Wheelock, who had revived and published Norman Clyde's "Close Ups of the High Sierra" thirty-five years earlier, stopped by my studio on his way back to southern California from Washington. During the course of conversation, Walt quietly mentioned that Norman Clyde had asked him to dedicate "Close Ups of the High Sierra" to his late wife "Winnie." However, Walt never included the requested dedication to Winifred Clyde in either the original or later editions of "Close Ups of the High Sierra," quite possibly because he thought it "too sweet" for a mountaineering guide. Two months following his visit, Walt passed away at the age of 88, and whatever reasons he may have had for not including Clyde's dedication in the original books will forever remain a mystery.

Not much is known about Winifred "Winnie" May Bolster Clyde, born on May 1, 1890 in Johnstown, New York. She moved to Pasadena, California with her family in 1903. Ten years later, she went north to Oakland, where she studied nursing and worked at the Alta Bates Sanitarium. According to her family, it was in the Bay Area that she met Norman Clyde approximately one year before they married. They were married in Pasadena on June 15, 1915. They spent their honeymoon in Santa Barbara, with Winnie's sister Roberta, and her husband, Ross Austin. Following the honeymoon, they returned to San Francisco by ferry, the most convenient form of transport between coastal

Norman and Winnie Clyde on their honeymoon in Santa Barbara, 1915
(Photo by Ross Austin, Eastern California Museum Collection)

cities at the time. She continued to work as a registered nurse while Clyde taught.

In odd contrast to the mountains that would later completely absorb Clyde's life until his death, much of his life with Winnie, as documented by family photo albums, was spent near the sea. Before she met Clyde, Winnie was photographed in a fine hat and coat, seated alone on the rocks at Land's End in San Francisco looking west, toward the ocean. Other photographs show the young couple strolling across the sand at Land's End, or sitting on the rocks watching the waves break upon the rugged northern California coastline.

It is believed that Winnie contracted pulmonary tuberculosis while working as a nurse in Oakland. When she became sick, Clyde looked after her as long as he could, until it became clear that she needed more care than he was able to provide. They returned to southern California where she was admitted to the La Vina Sanitarium in Altadena, a small community located along the front range of the San Gabriel Mountains near her family's home in Pasadena. According to members of her family, Winnie Clyde actually died on February 14, 1919, however, her mother may have changed the date of her death to February 13 for religious reasons. There is much speculation among family members as to why the date may have been changed from Valentine's Day to the preceding day, but the real reason still remains unclear.

Not long after her death, Norman Clyde lost touch with Winnie's family and never attempted to contact them again. He moved to the east side of the Sierra Nevada and became fully absorbed in his lifelong obsession with climbing. He never talked about Winnie to anyone and most people who knew him assumed he had never been married. In fact, only a few of the mountaineers who climbed with Clyde in the Sierra Nevada knew he had been married, but never knew what happened to his wife or what her name was. Clyde never remarried and was never known to have been romantically linked to another woman.

It wasn't until 1990, on a visit to the Eastern California Museum in Independence, that the missing puzzle piece was put into place by Winnie's nephew, Mr. Walter Bolster of Sacramento. While visiting the museum, Mr. Bolster had a brief encounter with an individual who insisted that Norman Clyde had never been married. Following this somewhat unpleasant interlude, Mr. Bolster obtained a copy of the Clyde marriage certificate as proof, which he forwarded to the museum for their collection.

Almost forty years after the fact, we honor Norman Clyde's request to dedicate "Close Ups of the High Sierra" to Winnie.

The Gilbert-Powell peaks, located at the head of the middle fork of Bishop Creek

"Close Ups"
of our High Sierra
Part III: *The 13,000-13,500-foot peaks*
By Norman Clyde

ALTHOUGH the majority of the finer peaks of the southern Sierra rise to elevations exceeding 13,500 feet, yet many of them do not attain that altitude, a considerable number being between 13,000 and 13,500 feet above sea-level. It might be observed, however, that height is only one element in the appraisal of a mountain, whether from a scenic or from a mountaineering standpoint. Mt. Whitney, for example, as fine a mountain as it may be, is excelled in picturesqueness by many lower mountains in the Sierra, and the ascent, except for the rarity of the air near

Temple Crag, one of the most spectacular of the 13,000-13,500-foot Sierra peaks

the summit, is generally conceded to be very easy.

Along the more southerly portion of the Great Western Divide, on the Kings-Kern Divide and along the main crest overlooking Owens Valley, there are a few peaks within the elevations specified in this sketch. To the southwest of Lone Pine Peak—west of the town of Lone Pine—is an unnamed peak, 13,016 feet in altitude. Although not a conspicuous one, it affords the best view to be had of Mt. Le Conte, whose line of jagged pinnacles towers to the south across a deep, narrow gorge; an excellent one of Mt. Langley, with sheer

Close Ups of the High Sierra as it appeared in the June 1928 issue
of "Touring Topics," published by the Automobile Club of Southern California
(Andy Zdon Collection)

INTRODUCTION
by Walt Wheelock

Norman Clyde, a name as legendary as that of Fremont or Muir. Norman Clyde, a man to whom the entire High Sierra was as familiar as ones own back yard. Norman Clyde, whose own life is much less known than that of the Greek heroes whose sagas he carried in his pack.

And how did this come about? For Clyde was a quiet, sometimes taciturn man, who often failed to leave a record of his achievements, and never boasted about his fabulous ascents. Yet, since he made his first trip to the top of Mt. Whitney, almost a half century ago, climbers have been finding his records on remote summits. A strong team of skilled rockclimbers will conquer a lonely spire, using the most modern of climbing gear and techniques and will summit with well-coordinated teamwork, only to find on a faded Kodak box, the record of a solo climb of more than six decades ago. Or, at the high point of a distant ridge will be found a small cairn, with no written record — obviously the work of man — and a climber will turn to his companion with, "Well, it looks like ours would have been a first ascent, if not for Norman Clyde." Later, upon discussing the route with him, Clyde would ponder a bit, ask a couple of questions about some difficult pitch encountered on the ascent, then admit he had been there scores of years ago.

Clyde was never one to bring up these mountaineering achievements. He would often sidestep them, or respond with his dry sense of humor, mentioning that he was in fact "350 years old," but he was never known to make a false statement when talking seriously. It was easy to tell the difference between his banter and his true accounts of his life and work. Research completely verifies the data and dates that he supplied.

Clyde's father, Charles Clyde was born in Antrim County in the north of Ireland in 1854. He migrated to this country at the age of seven. Clyde's mother, born Belle (Isabel) Purvis, was a native of Butler, a small city about thirty miles north of Pittsburgh. Charles and Belle were married at Butler and took up residence in Philadelphia, where Norman Asa Clyde, the first of nine children, was born the following year, on April 8, 1885. His father was a self-taught clergyman of the Covenanter sect of the Presbyterian faith.

When Clyde was three, the family moved to Ohio. His father served at a number of small churches, seldom staying more than a year at any one parsonage. Apparently the independence of thought that was later to dictate Clyde's flight to the mountains was honestly inherited. Eventually, his family moved to Glengarry County, near Ottawa, and Clyde remembered arriving there on the Queen's Jubilee Day (May 24, 1897).

Clyde lived there from the time he was twelve until he was seventeen. He could fish and hunt, practically in his own backyard, and soon became expert in both. His father, being self-taught and an avid student of the classics, took care of his son's schooling at home. Subsequently, Clyde learned Latin and Greek almost as early as he did his native tongue.

His father was stricken with pneumonia and passed away at the age of 46. His mother gathered up her flock and returned to western Pennsylvania. Clyde enrolled in Geneva College at Beaver Falls, but as he had no formal schooling, he had several deficiencies to make up at the prep level. Graduating with a degree in Classic Literature from Geneva in June, 1909, he immediately started west. He taught at several small rural schools across the country, including Fargo, North Dakota, and Mt. Pleasant, Utah. One summer was spent at the University of Wisconsin, John Muir's alma mater; another on a cattle spread in Utah.

Deciding that he needed more education to progress in the teaching field, he enrolled at the University of California at Berkeley in 1911. Summers were spent in the mountains and in teaching at summer schools. One was at Elko, Nevada, where he spent his spare time climbing the Humboldt Range.

At the end of two years at the university, Clyde found that he still lacked one course in Romance Drama and his thesis. He balked at the drama course, maintaining that Italian plays should be read in Italian, French dramas in French — neither in English. He could see no sense in struggling with a thesis which no one would ever read, so he quietly left the university without completing his master's degree.

During the next dozen years, the details of Clyde's life are rather sketchy, both in and out of the mountains. We know that he taught in a number of small schools in central and northern California. He remembered teaching near Stockton, and he spent a year each at Mt. Shasta and Weaverville. From his mountaineering notes, he must have spent some time in Arizona. Sometime during this period, he married a young lady from Pasadena. This is one part of his life that he refused to discuss. It is known that they lived together for three years and that she passed away from tuberculosis. It is apparent that he felt a deep love for his bride, and undoubtedly her passing was a strong factor in shaping his character.

In the field of mountaineering, we have a few more records. He was in Yosemite in 1914, where he first met up with the Sierra Club, joining with them on a trip to Tuolumne. Clyde became a member of the Club that year. After leading the annual Club outing, he traveled south along the backbone of the Sierra with a packtrain run by Charley Robinson, an old-time Sierra packer. The trip ended at Lone Pine, and Clyde made the first of his fifty ascents of Mt. Whitney at this time. Records show twelve ascents of Mt. Shasta, including three in four days. On one of these he set a record that only has been broken once since that time. Another page of his notes lists seven ascents of Weaver Bally in the Trinity country of northern California.

Clyde accompanied the Sierra Club on their trip from Yosemite through Evolution Valley in 1920, during which time he

Clyde on the summit of Mt. Cleveland in Glacier National Park
(Eastern California Museum Collection)

made several first ascents. It was on this trip that he carried the
first of his famous big packs. Leaving the Valley a couple of days
behind the Sierra Club and not knowing for sure whether he
could catch up with the group, he took along sufficient food. As
he swung by Camp Curry, he noticed a platform scale, and
weighed his pack in at seventy-five pounds. The next night was
spent with a survey crew that he had met on the trail. They
seemed amazed at the size of the pack (at that time Clyde
weighed 140 pounds) and kept commenting about it. In the
morning, one of the crew suggested that he might have trouble
finding the packtrain and suggested that he take along a few
extra cans of food that they had. Another offered a couple of
other items. As later companions were to find out, Clyde never
turned down free supplies. The group kept offering him more,
while relating the dangers of being caught in the wilderness without food. After they had loaded him down with an additional

twenty pounds, he was allowed to go his way. It was not until the next day that Clyde realized it had all been a gag to see how much he could carry, but it is still a question as to which side came out ahead with the gag.

In the fall of 1924, Clyde was appointed principal of the high school at Independence in Owens Valley. Situated at the foot of Mt. Williamson, probably the most magnificent of all of the 14,000-footers, it was within easy driving distance of most of the approaches to the High Sierra. Every weekend, he would lock up his school and dash off for the peaks. The record for 1925 shows that he logged 48 climbs, of which exactly half were first ascents. Only on six of the total number did he have a climbing companion. The following year, the number of ascents was boosted to sixty — that is sixty that have been recorded. Clyde was exploring the range at a rate that far surpassed the records of Brewer, Clarence King or John Muir.

However, a number of the townspeople were not so impressed by this record. Certainly Clyde was an excellent instructor and he controlled the wild youths of this mountain valley like they had never been controlled before. But a school teacher, especially a principal, was supposed to be an important man in the social and cultural life of the community. On Sunday, he should be attending one of the local churches. On Friday night, if there was a school social function, the principal was an honored, if captive, guest. Many of the neighbors were openly stating that Independence High needed a principal that would act as a principal should, rather than a crazy mountain climber.

Then came Halloween of 1927. Rumor had it that the boys were going to play many a prank on the school facilities and it seemed that these were not to be harmless pranks. Clyde stationed himself nearby, armed with a .38-caliber revolver. As a carload of youths drove onto the school grounds, he challenged them. They refused to stop, so he fired a warning shot. Apparently the rowdies believed that Clyde could be bluffed and kept on. He fired a second shot, which ricocheted fragments of lead onto the car. The hoodlums left and soon were telling the story all over the town, taking the whole thing as a huge joke.

Not so their parents — they waited upon the sheriff and demanded a warrant for attempted murder. The sheriff turned down this request, saying that if Clyde had attempted murder, it would have been murder, as he was the best pistol shot in the county. Next a request was made for a complaint charging illegal use of firearms. After a few days, Clyde resigned; all charges were dropped and Independence had traded its most colorful principal for a teacher that would act as a teacher should act.

No longer tied to regular employment, he plunged into a full-time study of the High Sierra. Within the next year a large number of articles poured from his pen, including the well-known series "Close Ups" of Our High Sierra that first appeared in Touring Topics (the predecessor to Westways) in the spring and summer of 1928.

His summers were spent climbing in the backcountry. At times Clyde would guide parties to the summit of difficult peaks and it made no difference if the climbers were a USGS party attempting to place a benchmark on an "unscaleable" summit or a lady peak-bagger; they made their peaks with Norman Clyde.

His winters were usually spent as a caretaker at a mountain resort. Thus, he was able to hole-in at such places as Glacier Point at Yosemite, Giant Forest at Sequoia, Parcher and Andrews camps on Bishop Creek, Glacier Lodge above Big Pine, and at Whitney Portal. Many were the times that Clyde rescued lost or snow-bound climbers, or if not called in time, located their bodies. His ability to locate wrecked planes had been the subject of numerous magazine stories. In 1939, his alma mater, Geneva College, awarded him a degree of Doctor of Science in appreciation of his mountain writings.

Well into his late seventies, Clyde still spent his summers acting as a guide on Sierra Club Base Camp trips and continued to lead private parties into his beloved Sierra. Much of the gruffness of his earlier years had disappeared, and his clear light blue eyes and pink, freshly shaven face gave him the appearance of an alpine gnome. He used to say that he would continue to climb the Sierra until the day he would just forget to come back.

During his last years, Clyde spent most of his time living at his old ranch house on Baker Creek, near Big Pine, California — a primitive three-room place with no electricity or plumbing. He used kerosene lanterns and the running water of a stream which flowed through a spring house. His home and adjoining arbor were covered with a canopy of grape vines and climbing roses.

Clyde spent part of each summer at Sierra Club base camps, where he would entertain at campfires with tales of his earlier years. He was always available to chat with those who wished to hear directly from him about those magnificent and legendary days in the Range of Light.

In his mid-eighties, Clyde was found to be suffering from an enlarged heart, and it became obvious that he would require more attention. So his last few years were spent in a rest home in Big Pine — until he set out for his final ascent on the twenty-third day of December, 1972.

Various newspaper accounts reported that Clyde had been buried in Tonopah, Nevada. Yet a final resting place in a mining town located in central Nevada seemed strange to those who knew him, in part because he rarely left the east side of the Sierra. Actually, a small party of mountaineers, namely Jules Eichorn, Smoke Blanchard with son Bob, and Nort Benner, quietly carried Clyde's ashes up Big Pine Creek to the peak that Norman Clyde looked out upon from his ranch window in Baker Creek. It was on the jagged crest of that peak, which would later bear his name, that Clyde's ashes were scattered in full view of the magnificent Sierra Nevada.

RECOLLECTIONS
by Glen Dawson

I was a young boy when I first met Norman Clyde. Though I don't remember exactly when I met him, I do know that on the Sierra Club High Trip of 1926 to Yellowstone National Park, my father left me in the care of Dr. Vernon Bailey and went off with Norman Clyde and others to climb the Grand Teton.

Norman Clyde lived much of his life in the Owens Valley and the Sierra Nevada. He came to Los Angeles once or twice a year and would use Dawson's Book Shop as his post office, bank, library and storage facility. He was about three years younger than my father, Ernest.

During the summer of 1927, I was again on the Sierra Club High Trip where I made my first High Sierra climb, an ascent of Table Mountain led by Norman Clyde, who at the time was still a high school principal in Independence.

On some of the High Trips, Norman was paid to assist on mountain climbs. Jules Eichorn and I usually preferred to climb on our own at our own pace, but Norman made himself available to us for advice and suggestions.

In 1931, Francis Farquhar invited me and Jules Eichorn to be part of the Palisade Climbing School with Norman Clyde and Robert Underhill. Norman was our guide in the ascents of what are now known as Starlight and Thunderbolt. Following the Palisades, five of us went to Mt. Whitney. Jules roped up with Norman and I with Robert Underhill. On August 16, 1931, we climbed the East Face of Mt. Whitney.

In 1932, Bestor Robinson organized a climb of El Picacho del Diablo, the highest peak in Baja California. Norman Clyde, Dick Jones, Walter Brem, Nathan Clark and I were invited to participate.

In 1933, Jules Eichorn, Dick Jones and I were asked to join the

The summit of El Picacho del Diablo in Baja, Mexico: Norman Clyde,
Nathan Clarke, Glen Dawson. Seated: Richard Jones and Walter Brem
(The Colby Library, Sierra Club)

search for Walter Starr Jr. We found indications of his being on
Michael Minaret. After the search was called off and most of us
had to leave, it was Norman who stayed on and found Starr's
body, which he interred in a great cairn of granite.

I always had to reduce my load of equipment to the bare
minimum to keep up with Norman. He could carry monumental
loads which included such items as a pistol, a shoe cobbler's out-
fit, sewing equipment, books, tools and kitchenware. Much of
this seemed unnecessary to me.

Once he visited us at our home in Los Angeles. The back end
of his car was piled high with camping gear and Norman admitted there was a mouse living in the back of his automobile. He
wasn't able to catch the mouse although his experiences trapping
martens in the High Sierra during the dead of winter were quite
successful.

Norman was always very polite and cooperative with me, perhaps because I was one of Ernest's sons. However, on occasion, Norman could be very persistent, stubborn, and unyielding. His published writings gave elegant details of his prodigious mountain climbing feats, while his personal letters expressed his opinions colorfully and definitely.

Norman wrote, rewrote and recycled his submissions to a wide variety of mostly obscure periodicals, but he had one good paying customer, Phil Townsend Hanna of Touring Topics, the Automobile Club of Southern California's original monthly magazine, and predecessor to Westways and Avenues. A bibliography or checklist of Clyde's published writings would certainly be a challenge to anyone willing to take on the task. One of my own most treasured items, is a four page off-print from the 1931 American Alpine Journal's "Difficult Peaks of the Sierra Nevada," which Norman inscribed to me.

There has been an increasing interest in the life and exploits of Norman Clyde. No one has had a closer identification with the summits of the High Sierra than Norman Clyde and no one will ever duplicate what he accomplished in his lifetime.

A HALF CENTURY OF CLIMBING
by Norman Clyde

1914 was the first year that I did any climbing of any account in the Sierra. Climbing at that time was what mountaineers sometimes term "free climbing." Ropes were seldom used and those that were, were not adequate and probably no one knew anything about the technique of using a rope in climbing. An ice axe was seldom or never seen. Any ice cutting that was done was usually done with some sort of a wood axe. As to foot gear, there was a tendency to wear at least moderately high boots. These were often of a very good grade and their owner was ofttimes quite proud of them. Often they were provided with Hungarian nails or hobnails. The former were fairly satisfactory until worn flat, so that the wearer was likely to do considerable skating around on smooth rocks.

In the twenties there was considerable change. Personally, I learned the technique of rope climbing from Swiss guides and the Canadian Alpine Club in the Canadian Rockies. Thereafter, I seldom did any serious climbing without carrying a standard seven-sixteenth-inch rope or lighter one, which I called an "emergency" rope and which was adequate for roping down; what was coming to be known as rappelling or for occasionally belaying. Ice axes were seen occasionally. A few climbers took to wearing boots provided with Swiss edge nails. Somewhat later, I changed to Tricouni nails. These were better on snow and ice than the edge nails, but not too satisfactory on smooth, hard rock. For rock climbing, I usually carried a pair of rubber-soled shoes — preferably crepe rubber — in my rucksack. Most Sierra climbers had some sort of rubber-soled shoes in reserve. The techniques of rope climbing gradually improved, also "hardware" climbing came more or less in vogue, particularly on the walls of Yosemite.

At first pitons were used merely as a safety precaution reserved for difficult pitches. Some climbers, however, came to depend more and more upon them, and were able to make climbs that otherwise would be impossible.

Later, in the matter of footgear, there was a gradual change from nailed soles to cleated rubber ones, at first to the Bramani design. Somewhat later a further change was made to the Vibram type, which came nearer to being an all-around satisfactory mountain climbing boot than any other boot yet produced. Climbers, who encountered much ice and snow may supplement these with crampons.

Today, climbers in the High Sierra may be roughly divided into several groups. One group, which may be the walkers, who seldom go past class 2 climbing. These often do not carry a rope. Another group is satisfied with class 3 and class 4 grades, seldom going beyond. These usually do and always should carry a rope and often carry along a few pitons and carabiners, to help themselves over a difficult pitch. If there is snow and ice, they add an ice axe. Lastly, are the technical rock climbers, who are not happy unless they encounter a liberal measure of class 5 and class 6 pitches.

All forms are legitimate if proper safety measures are followed. There is room for all. Some may not think "hardware" climbing is justified on account of the supposed risks involved. Properly equipped and careful climbers, however, incur less dangerous exposure on class 5 and class 6 routes than untrained men inadvertently may on class 3 or even class 2. Everyone to his taste. "De gustibus non disputandum est," as the old Latin proverb goes.

Mt. Goddard (Photo by Norman Clyde, Wynne Benti Collection)

The most charming lake of the Sierra;
rugged encircling mountains,
the sound of falling water,
picturesque islands and rugged shores;
the deep blue color of the lake itself.
By night, the moon is obscured by clouds
and the mountains are darkly
reflected in the lake.

Journal entry
Rae Lake

14,000-FOOT PEAKS

North Palisade

Few Californians know even the names of the 14,000-foot peaks of the Sierra Nevada, their knowledge of them being usually limited to the fact that Mt. Whitney is the highest mountain in the continental United States. Few are aware that there are ten others, all of which have at least one feature of interest.

They are either scenically attractive, afford exceptionally fine views from their summits, offer mountaineering inducements or possess all of these characteristics. All are found along the axis of the range from a point west of Lone Pine to one in the same direction from Big Pine. All may be said to be included in three groups which we may call those of Mt. Whitney, Mt. Williamson and the Palisades, from the most prominent mountain in each of them.

In this sketch we shall begin with the first of these. Many appear to be disappointed with the views ordinarily obtained of Mt. Whitney. Viewed from the Owens Valley to the east, other, considerably lower peaks, due to their position, seem to rival or even exceed it in height. Furthermore, from the Kern region to the west, the comparatively gentle slope of that face of the mountain appears to rob it of spectacular features. However, both of these estimates appear to be in some degree unwarranted, for as one approaches Mt. Whitney from the east, its series of granite pinnacles stand in beautiful perspective at the head of Lone Pine

Canyon, a fine gorge walled in on either side throughout most of its length by high granite cliffs. If one surveys Mt. Whitney from the summit of any of the peaks of the Great Western Divide, the depth and the breadth of the Kern Basin, seem to impart to it a grandeur that it appears to lack when beheld from nearer points in that direction.

But it is from the seldom-trodden vantage points that Mt. Whitney is most imposing. From Lone Pine Peak, Mts. Mallory and Irvine, Le Conte and Langley to the east and south; and from Mts. Russell, Barnard and others to the north, Mt. Whitney is spectacular to a degree that would surprise those who have seen it only from the usual viewpoints.

The panorama beheld from Mt. Whitney is one of great extent and magnificence. To the north it extends along the axis of the range to the mountains of Yosemite; to the west it looks across the Kern Basin to the castellated Kaweahs and the jagged line of the Kern-Kaweah Divide; to the south, over gradually lowering forest-clad mountains; to the east and southeast, over a multitude of arid ranges and desert valleys.

Mt. Whitney is regarded by mountaineers as being a remarkably easy ascent. From the west, aside from a chimney of about a thousand feet, it is a walk up comparatively gentle slopes. From the east it demands more endurance, requiring a person to be in good condition to climb to timberline and return without suffering from overexertion.

The last of the high pinnacles on the ridge running south from Mt. Whitney is called Mt. Muir. It attains an elevation of 14,025 feet. As one comes up the Mt. Whitney Trail from the east, its sheer face and sharp summit are very striking. The summit commands an excellent view, especially of the rugged mountains to the southeast. It rises several hundred feet above the trail that winds along to the west of it, and necessitates a short but interesting rockclimb to reach it.

A few miles to the southeast of Mt. Whitney is Mt. Langley, 14,042 feet in elevation and the southernmost of the 14,000-foot

Middle Palisade
(Photo by Norman Clyde, Eastern California Museum Collection)

Peaks shown:

Sawtooth Pk.
Mt. Langley
Mt. Le Conte
Mt. Mallory
Peak 13,800
Mt. Irvine
Lone Pine Peak
Mt. Muir
Mt. Whitney
Mt. Russell
Mt. Kaweah
Red Kaweah
Black Kaweah
Triple Divide Peak
Milestone Mtn.
Table Mtn.
Thunder Mtn.
Mt. Jordan
Mt. Barnard
Mt. Williamson
M. Tyndall
Junction Peak
Mt. Keith
Mt. Stanford
Deerhorn Mtn.
Mt. Bradley
University Pk.
East Vidette
Mt. Ericsson
North Guard
Mt. Brewer
South Guard
Mt. Genevra

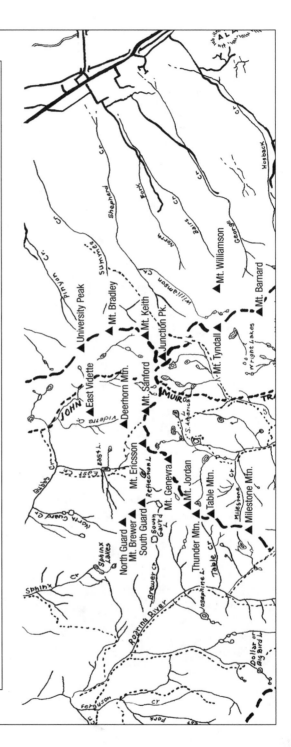

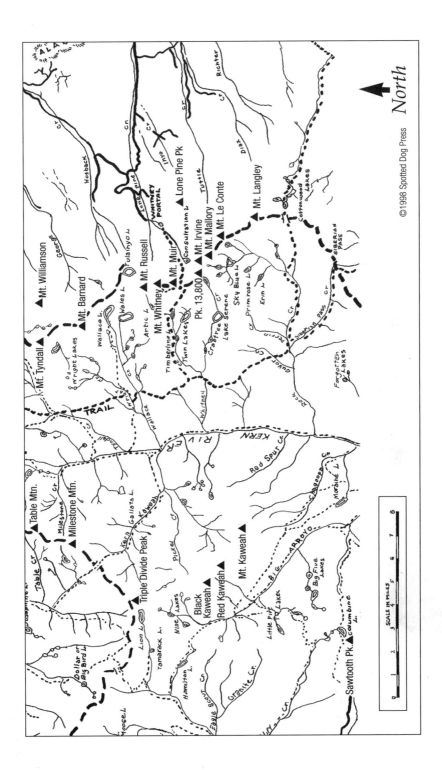

ALA

Hosback Cr

George Cr

Lone Pine Cr

Lone Pine Cr

Inyo Cr

Richter Cr

▲ Mt. Williamson

▲ Mt. Barnard

WHITNEY PORTAL

▲ Consultation L

▲ Lone Pine Pk

Tuttle Cr

Diaz Cr

▲ Mt. Tyndall

Wales L

Artic L

▲ Mt. Russell

▲ Mt. Whitney

▲ Mt. Muir

▲ Mt. Irvine

▲ Mt. Mallory

▲ Mt. Le Conte

▲ Mt. Langley

Cottonwood Lakes

Wright Lakes

Wallace L

Wallace Cr

Timberline L

Twin Lakes

Pk. 13,800

Crabtree Cr

Lake Serene

Sky Blue L

Primrose L

Erin L

SIBERIAN PASS

TRAIL

Tyndall Cr

Wallace Cr

Kern Cr

Siberian Pass Cr

Forgotten Lakes

Whitney Cr

Guyot Cr

Rock Cr

Table Cr

Milestone Cr

Table Mtn. ▲

Milestone Mtn. ▲

Triple Divide Peak ▲

Kern Gallots L

Picket Cr

KERN RIVER

Red Spur Cr

Moraine L

Big Arroyo Cr

Lion L

Dollar or Big Bird L

Tamarack L

Nine Lakes

Black Kaweah ▲

Red Kaweah ▲

Mt. Kaweah ▲

Hamilton L

Eagle Scout Cr

Granite Cr

Little Five Lakes

Big Five Lakes

Sawtooth Pk. ▲

Columbine L

Moose L

SCALE IN MILES

1 2 3 4 5 6 7 8

North

©1998 Spotted Dog Press

peaks of the Sierra. In form it is similar to Mt. Whitney, as it slopes up gradually from the south and the southwest and breaks off in sheer precipices to the north and east. The view from its summit is very good but does not equal that from those farther to the north. The ascent from the south is extremely easy — in fact, a horse can be ridden to the summit from that direction. From the northwest it offers somewhat of a rock climb.

Immediately to the north of Mt. Whitney across a deep cirque, is Mt. Russell, 14,190 feet in altitude. It is a fine craggy mountain, one that delights the heart of a mountaineer, and has been ascended fewer times than any other 14,000-foot peak in the Sierra Nevada. The ascent can be made from several directions, but is foolhardy for any but experienced mountaineers to climb it.

Mt. Russell's summit possesses one of the finest views obtainable of Mt. Whitney, as it looks directly across a chasm-like depression to the precipitous northern face of the latter. The view northward along the crest of the range westward over the Kern is magnificent.

Mt. Williamson, about twelve miles north of Mt. Whitney, is one of the finest of the 14,000-foot peaks. Being only slightly lower than Mt. Whitney – 14,384 feet – and rising directly from the valley floor, it is probably the most spectacular mountain of all the ranges viewed from Owens Valley. Its handsome, deeply-fluted, cathedral-like mass is especially picturesque from the east and the north, while from the crest of the Sierra it is one of the most conspicuous peaks and can be seen from almost every prominent elevation. The panorama visible from its summit is one of the finest in the Sierra, equaling, if not surpassing, that from Mt. Whitney, while its ascent is considerably more difficult than that of its loftier neighbor to the south.

A mile or so west of Mt. Williamson is Mt. Tyndall, (14,025'). Its steep eastern face can be seen from Owens Valley, just to the north of the former. A fine view is to be had from its summit, especially of the great amphitheater of lofty mountains that encircle the upper Kern basin. The ascent is an easy matter, despite

Split Mountain (Photo by Tom Ross, Wynne Benti Collection)

Clarence King's hair-raising story. From the northwest, the climber works his way up some 2,000 feet of talus rock and then along about 200 yards of narrow arete to the summit.

For some forty miles northward along the crest from Mt. Williamson, there occur no 14,000-foot mountains. At this distance from it is the Palisade group, one of the finest in the Sierra. From the higher peaks all along the axis of the range from Mt. Whitney in the south to Mt. Lyell in the north, this cluster of serrated pinnacles and jagged ridges is conspicuous. Their southern faces rise abruptly — in most places sheer; their northern ones, with the exception of Split Mountain, are even more vertical. The North and Middle Palisades have been scaled from the south only; the South Palisade (Split Mountain) from the north only; Mt. Sill usually from the north.

The most beautiful mountain of these and one of the most beautiful in the Sierra is the North Palisade. Whether one scans its jagged pinnacles from the south across granite gorges or across the Palisade Glacier and the basin to the north; it is one of the most striking peaks in the Sierra Nevada. Probably the view from its summit equals in scope and magnificence that obtained from any peak in the range and without being unusually hazardous or difficult, it is sufficiently so to render it interesting to the most skilled mountaineer.

About a mile to the east of the North Palisade is Mt. Sill, approximately 14,200 feet in elevation. It is an impressive mountain from the north and northeast, its sheer cliffs hundreds of feet in height facing these directions. It can be seen from Owens Valley in the vicinity of Big Pine. The view from its summit is fine but not quite equal to that of the North Palisade. Although a comparatively easy climb from the south, few have ever made the ascent. It can also be scaled from the Palisade Glacier by those experienced in rock climbing.

Somewhat farther to the southeast is the Middle Palisade, 14,049 feet in elevation, the second of the group in scenic beauty and possibly the first in mountaineering difficulty. From the

south it presents an imposing array of crags and pinnacles; from
the north it is even more impressive as it rises in sheer cliffs above
a steeper glacier at the head of a deep canyon. There is an especially fine view of it looking up the south fork of Big Pine Creek
about a half-mile west of Glacier Lodge. The panorama seen
from its summit is inferior to that of those of this group already
mentioned, but contains more of a great eastern escarpment of
the Sierra. It has been scaled few times and only from the south;
it is essentially a crag-and-chimney climb and is not recommend-
ed for novices. The summit itself is a ragged knife-edge about a
hundred yards in length.

A few miles farther to the southeast, so far as sometimes to
be regarded as not belonging to this group, is the South Palisade
or Split Mountain, 14,051 feet in elevation. It is visible from the
high peaks to the south and is the most colorful of the 14,000-foot
peaks, the great cliffs of its southern and eastern faces displaying
broad bands and extensive areas of red, orange, brown, and other
tints, while the summit forms a great capping of dark gray granite. It is very striking from Owens Valley, a few miles north of
Independence.

The panorama seen from its summit ranks among the fine
ones of the range. It is scaleable from the north only as the other
faces of the mountain are sheer cliffs. From this direction it is
very readily ascended, but due to its inaccessibility few have ever
stood on the summit.

A deep winding chimney.
Wonderful views in every direction
but the upper Kings and Kern were enveloped
by a dense thundercloud, which soon came
bearing down upon the peak.
Heavy snow pellets drove against us while
thunder and lightening played about us.
The rocks became wet and a stream began
to course down the chimney.
Drenched and cold.

Journal entry
An ascent of Black Kaweah

13,500 TO 14,000-FOOT PEAKS

Mt. Brewer

Both from a scenic and from a mountaineering standpoint many of the finest peaks of the Sierra Nevada range from 13,000 feet above sea-level to a trifle less than 14,000 feet. It seems to the writer that from neither of these viewpoints is the Sierra Nevada adequately appreciated, for the Sierra is not only one of the most imposing ranges in the United States en masse but also contains many individual peaks of great beauty and numbers whose ascent requires considerable mountaineering skill and daring. In both of these respects there are probably more noteworthy peaks within the range of elevation spoken of above than any other of similar radius in the Sierra. Beginning with the most southerly in the range, I shall briefly review some of the most outstanding of them.

As one looks westward from the vicinity of Lone Pine he observes a jagged line of pinnacles along the crest of the Sierra, that gradually increases in height from the south to the north, to the highest which attains an elevation of 13,960 feet. This is Mt. Le Conte. If it is impressive when beheld from Owens Valley, it is much more so when seen from nearby peaks across deep cirques which greatly enhance the striking appearance of this array of giant pinnacles that rise sheer for hundreds of feet. In the matter of ascent it ranks among the more difficult peaks of the Sierra and has been climbed but twice. Nearby to the north and northwest,

Mts. Mallory, Irvine and Peak 13,800 have been scaled but few times — the last but once. The first two are especially noteworthy on account of the excellent views that they afford of the precipitous eastern front of Mt. Whitney.

From almost any of the higher elevations of the southern Sierra, one can descry the splendid group of the Kaweahs, situated westward from Mt. Whitney across the Kern Basin. They attain an average elevation of about 13,700 feet and form one of the most beautiful and spectacular groups in all of the Sierra. They include Mt. Kaweah, and the Red, Gray and Black Kaweahs. To the north, the sheer walls of all of them rise above a great cirque; to the south and west, three of them have an easy approach up one face, with the exception of the Black Kaweah which is sheer on all sides. In their beautifully serrated lines they are among the most conspicuous mountains in the Sierra; in richness of color, they are the finest in the Kern region and among the finest in the range. In all, except the Black Kaweah — which in most lights is a gleaming black — the prevailing color is a rich red.

Like the Palisades farther to the north, they have the distinction of being picturesque, no matter from what direction they may be viewed; or whether from far or near. Close at hand, they are especially striking from the Five Lakes Basin and the Chagoopa Plateau to the south, and from the elevations about the upper Kern-Kaweah to the north. From almost all points in the upper Kern region, this cluster of peaks stands out superbly picturesque, while seen from the high peaks far up the range, they form one of the most beautiful landmarks in the Sierra. All of the main peaks but the Black Kaweah are easy of ascent. The last is regarded as one of the most difficult and dangerous peaks of the high Sierra and its summit can be reached only by climbing a long chimney running up its southern face.

Slightly to the west of the Kaweahs, extending north and south past them, is the Kern-Kaweah or Great Western Divide. It was once the main crest of the Sierra and is now remarkable for the extreme ruggedness and variation of the forms of the peaks of

University Peak
(Photo by Norman Clyde, Eastern California Museum Collection)

which it is composed. It is a long line of spirey, pyramidal and mesa-like peaks that are extremely impressive as they stand silhouetted against the blue sky, or as billowy clouds hover about their ragged crest. The most noteworthy of these is Milestone Mountain. It is essentially a pyramid surmounted by a slender flat-topped spire several hundred feet in height and attaining an altitude of 13,643 feet above sea-level. Apparently inaccessible on all sides, it is actually so on three of them, but the western side — despite its formidable wall-like appearance – can be scaled with comparative ease. This vulnerable face can be approached from the south, the north – with difficulty – or from the east by crossing the crest on either side of the great obelisk that forms the summit. It is regarded as one of the finest viewpoints in the Sierra. To the south, the Kaweahs; to the east, across the Kern Basin, the great peaks of the main crest of the Sierra; to the north and northeast, those of the Kings-Kern Divide form a panorama of the most rugged sublimity.

Northward a short distance from Milestone Mountain is Table Mountain, 13,646 feet in elevation. It is a great flat-topped mountain whose sides in most places seem almost vertical.

Peaks shown:

Mt. Rixford
Mt. Gould
Independence Peak
Dragon Peak
Kearsarge Peak
Mt. Gardiner
Black Peak
Diamond Peak
Mt. Clarence King
Baxter Peak
Colosseum Mtn.
Mt. Perkins
Arrow Mtn.
Mt. Pinchot
Striped Mtn.
Cardinal Mtn.
Split Mtn.
Bolton Brown Mtn.
Birch Mtn.
The Thumb
Middle Palisade
Mt. Sill
North Palisade

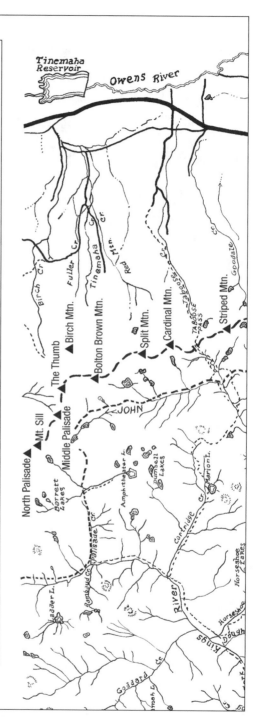

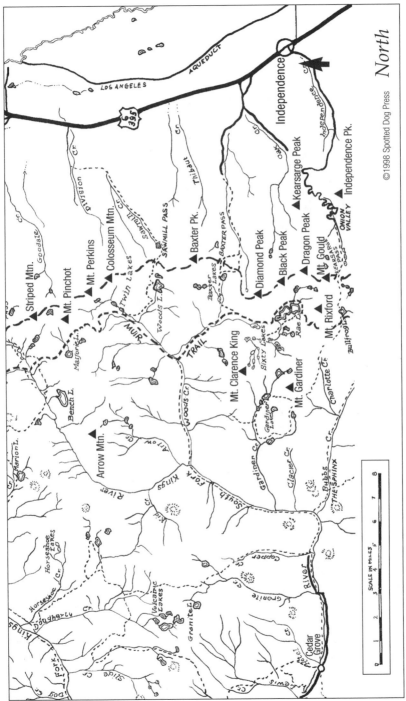

©1998 Spotted Dog Press

North

Although comparatively easy of ascent from the south along narrow shelves and up a rocky chimney, it has been climbed but few times. It can also be surmounted by forcing one's way up a precipitous chimney on its northern face and over several hundred feet of broken, steeply sloping wall above it, but this route is likely to entail a good deal of snow and perhaps some ice climbing. The summit slants down gently to the south and it is both novel and interesting to walk across it, or around its border that drops away in most places in sheer precipices.

In striking contrast to the mesa-like form of Table Mountain is the slender pyramid of Thunder Mountain (13,578') only a short distance to the north of it — one of the finest examples in the Sierra of what one might call the Gothic type. Its summit tapers to three slender spires, one of which is somewhat higher than the others and only a few feet in diameter at its highest point. It commands an excellent view and has probably been scaled but twice.

Northward a few miles from Thunder Mountain is Mt. Brewer, 13,555 feet in height. It can be readily climbed from the northeast, the south and the west, and possesses one of the best views obtainable in the Sierra. From the north especially it is a remarkably beautiful peak, its broadly pyramidal lines and vertical northern face being visible far up the range, and together with the North and South Guards on either side of it, forms one of the most imposing groups in the Sierra.

Along the Kings-Kern Divide, slightly to the south of Mt. Brewer, are numbers of lofty peaks, the finest of which is Mt. Stanford, 13,983 feet in altitude. Its wide, massive form is seen to best advantage from the north across the great amphitheater in that direction, but its southwestern cliffs are very impressive from the western portion of the upper Kern Basin. It has twin peaks of almost equal height, the northern one being perhaps a few feet the higher. The most southerly of these can be readily scaled from the Upper Kern, but few care to traverse the ragged knife-edge that connects it with the more northerly one. Other worthwhile

peaks along the Kings-Kern Divide are Junction Peak (13,903')
and Mt. Ericsson (13,625'). Neither has been climbed frequently
and the former affords good rock climbing up a knife-edge from
the east; the latter, up its eastern face.

Along the main crest to the east of the upper Kings
amphitheater are two peaks over 13,500 feet in altitude; Mt. Keith
(13,990') and University Peak (13,588'). The former can easily be
climbed from Junction Pass; the latter can be scaled from Bullfrog
Lake, Vidette Meadow to the west, or from the Matlock Lakes and
the head of a canyon to the east. The view obtained from the
summit is extremely fine. University Peak is a very beautiful and
imposing mountain when seen from Kearsarge Peak to the northeast and from Independence Peak to the east. From University
Peak to Split Mountain , a distance of some fifteen miles in an air-
line, there occur no peaks with an altitude of 13,500 feet or over.
Just to the north of the last named are several seldom-climbed
ones, including Bolton Brown Mountain, Birch Mountain, The
Thumb and others.

In the northern portion of the Palisade group are two unusually fine ones in Mt. Winchell and Agassiz Needle (renamed Mt.
Agassiz). Both are scaleable from the Palisade Glacier; the former
being an excellent but not dangerous rock climb; the latter, a comparatively easy one. Agassiz Needle can be scaled up its eastern
face — a somewhat hazardous feat — and up its western slope, a
very easy one. Both afford superb views, especially of the Palisades
and northeast across the Palisade amphitheater.

Some fifteen miles to the northwest of the Palisades is the
Evolution group, an unusually interesting one containing a dozen
or more peaks surrounding a basin about six miles in length of the
same name. The best of these are Mts. Goddard and Darwin. The
broad, dark cone of the first, 13,841 feet in elevation, is a conspicuous landmark far to the north and the south along the crest of the
range. Due to its central and somewhat isolated position at the
southwestern end of Evolution Basin, it possesses one of the most
extensive views that can be had in the Sierra — one commanding

Bear Creek Spire (Photo by Norman Clyde, Eastern California Museum Collection)

the main axis of the range from Mt. Whitney to Mt. Lyell. The ascent is rather easy and can be made from the Evolution Basin to the north; the upper San Joaquin to the west and from the headwaters of Goddard Creek to the south.

Along the crest to the northeast of the basin is the great, flat-topped Mt. Darwin. Its walls are vertical almost everywhere and can be scaled from only two directions — across a glacier on its northern flank and along a knife-edge to the summit; up a tangle of chimneys on its southwestern face and thence by the same arete to the top. The highest point of the mountain is a slender turret just to the east of the main peak. Few have ascended the latter and still fewer the former. Mt. Darwin is considered to be one of the difficult mountains of the Sierra, and one possessing a very fine view.

As one looks northwestward from the summit of Mt. Darwin, he descries, within a distance of ten miles, a rather solitary peak rising from the verge of a wide, timberless basin mostly above an elevation of 11,000 feet. It is Mt. Humphreys. The mountain possesses an unusually stern and almost forbidding aspect. It is generally rated as one of the most difficult of the higher peaks of the Sierra Nevada, and although comparatively accessible, only about twenty-five humans have stood on its summit.

Northward a few miles from Mt. Humphreys is Mt. Tom, a beautiful, symmetrical mountain when viewed from the summit of Mt. Humphreys, the South Fork of Bishop Creek, Owens Valley or from the summit of Bear Creek Spire and other peaks to the northwest. Its richness of coloring, chiefly soft reds and browns, is very pleasing to the eye. The ascent presents no mountaineering difficulties, but is rather long, as the usual starting points are at comparatively low elevations.

To the northwest of Mt. Tom, across a profound gorge looms a sharp, pyramidal mountain, 13,708 feet in elevation. This is Bear Creek Spire, perhaps the finest of a number of peaks that encircle a treeless, granite basin containing Lake Italy. This basin is locked away in the Sierra in such a fashion that few have ever seen it. Lake Italy is a beautiful lake with rugged granite peaks springing up in every direction. Except for a few stunted albicaulis pines clinging to slopes with unusually favorable exposures, the valley is entirely devoid of trees.

Bear Creek Spire rises at the northeastern corner of the basin. Perhaps the most striking views of it are form the north, up Little Lakes Basin. It is an unusually impressive mountain of the Matterhorn type. On all sides, except the west, it drops away in almost vertical walls hundreds of feet in height. The summit itself is a single monolith only a few feet in diameter from which these jagged aretes radiate in true Matterhorn fashion. It has been scaled twice up its western face. On that side it slopes up gradually until within about a hundred and fifty feet of the summit, where a rock wall of considerable difficulty must be negotiated. The last rock, projecting above a narrow knife-edge with a drop of five hundred feet in one direction and one hundred fifty in the other, being of rather smooth granite and reaching a height that one can scarcely reach over and with no holds on its flanks except one or two shallow cup-like depressions, requires steady nerves.

The view obtained from this circumscribed perch is superb. To the east, across deep gorges, is Mt. Tom; to the south, beyond others, is the lofty and commanding form of Mt. Humphreys; to the southwest, Seven Gables, Mt. Hilgard and other rugged peaks; to the west, across Lake Italy Basin, Mt. Gabb; to the northwest, the group containing Mts. Dade, Abbot and Mills.

Another handsome mountain as one looks up the Rock Creek Basin is Mt. Dade. To the north it breaks away in sheer cliffs at whose base lies a small glacier. It can be readily climbed from Italy Basin, which is reached from upper Rock Creek by crossing a saddle to the east of the peak. It has been ascended only a few times, although the view from its summit is a very good one. It looks directly across Italy Basin to Seven Gables and far north and south along the crest of the range.

West of Mt. Dade, and joined to it by a sharp knife-edge is Mt. Abbot (13,736′). It can be ascended by scrambling up a chimney on its southern face and may possibly be climbed from the head-waters of Rock Creek. To the west of Italy Basin and occupying a somewhat isolated position is Mt. Gabb (13,701'). It is an easy climb and its summit commands a fine prospect. The fact that none of the Abbot group is climbed frequently is due largely to their standing to the side of the main lines of travel in the Sierra Nevada. They rise in a somewhat remote and sequestered region which possesses a certain charm all its own. In every direction they over-look high granite basins for the most part above the timberline. As one looks up upper Rock Creek Basin, Bear Creek Spire and Mts. Dade and Abbot form a superb skyline of jagged peaks.

To the southeast of upper Rock Creek Basin is Mt. Morgan (13,739'). It also has been climbed but a few times, notwithstand-ing the fact that its summit affords a sublime view across great gorges, far down the crest of the Sierras; northward past the rich-ly colored mountains above Convict Lake to the Yosemite Mountains beyond them.

With the above peaks, the 13,500-foot peaks of the Sierra ter-minate, the loftiest of those to the north being slightly over 13,000 feet in elevation. Although less than 14,000 feet in elevation, they are mountains of which California may well be proud, for their picturesqueness, for the magnificent views obtained from their summits and for the opportunities for strenuous but beautiful mountaineering which they afford.

Perfect solitude.
Morning brook; delightful cool breeze;
silent, stately sunflecked trees.
Scene of fresh green and warm browns
and reds with a blue sky overhead.

Journal entry
Red Wood Glen

13,000 TO 13,500-FOOT PEAKS

Although the majority of the finer peaks of the southern Sierra rise to elevations exceeding 13,500 feet, many of them do not attain that altitude, with a considerable number being between 13,000 and 13,500 feet above sea level. It might be observed, however, that height is only one element in the appraisal of a mountain, whether from a scenic or from a mountaineering standpoint. Mt. Whitney, for example, as fine a mountain as it may be, is excelled in picturesqueness by many lower mountains in the Sierra, and the ascent, except for the rarity of air near the summit, is generally conceded to be very easy.

Along the more southerly portion of the Great Western Divide, on the Kings-Kern Divide and along the main crest over looking Owens Valley, there are a few peaks within the elevation specified in this sketch. To the southwest of Lone Pine Peak — is an unnamed peak, 13,016 feet in altitude. Although not a conspicuous one, it affords the best view to be had of Mt. Le Conte, whose line of jagged pinnacles towers to the south across a deep, narrow gorge; an excellent view of Mt. Langley, with sheer northern and eastern precipices beyond it; of Mts. Mallory and Irvine to the west, and of Mt. Whitney to the northwest. The summit is a ragged knife-edge that presents some difficulties to the climber and has been scaled probably but once. On the Kings-Kern Divide there are two which might be included.

Mt. Genevra (13,037') and Mt. Jordan (13,136') are both easy ascents, and being located near the junction of the Kings-Kern and the Kern-Kaweah divides, possess excellent views of both as well as the great amphitheater to the north.

Cutting northward from about the middle of the Kings-Kern Divide is Deerhorn Mountain, a beautiful peak consisting of a line of granite spires, the highest of which is 13,440 feet in elevation. It is one of the finest "crag" mountains of the Sierra. The best view of it is obtained from the vicinity of Bullfrog Lake looking southward past the East Vidette and across the amphitheater, from which it stands out as one of the most striking peaks along the divide, although others exceed it considerably in height. Its craggy structure is seen to best advantage to the south of Harrison Pass and the top of Mt. Ericsson. Its summit affords the best view obtainable of the crags of Mt. Ericsson, immediately to the south across a bow-shaped cirque. Although probably scaled but once, the ascent is not especially difficult for one experienced in rock-climbing.

Mt. Brewer, one of the most attractive of Sierra peaks, has a peak on either flank, called respectively the North and South Guards. The former, 13,304 feet in altitude, is a fine rock-climb, and has had only one ascent, and that dubious, as the climber did not scale a granite monolith some twenty feet in height which may be the highest point and which, without hand or foot-holds, leans in an embarrassing way over a five-hundred foot precipice. There is also some difference of opinion as to whether the South Guard is Spire 12,964 or Peak 13,232 to the south of the former. Both are easily climbed and both afford good views. The first has probably been climbed but once.

Between Mt. Keith and University Peak on the main crest to the east of the upper Kings amphitheater is Mt. Bradley, 13,320 feet in elevation. It is a somewhat impressive peak as seen from Owens Valley, near Independence, and can be climbed from that side if one has sufficient patience to work his way up the rugged, trail-less canyon of Piñon Creek. Most of the few ascents that have been made, however, were from the upper portion of Center Basin to the west of the peak. It commands an excellent view.

Just to the north of Kearsarge Pass is Mt. Gould (13,001'), worthy of noting on account of its accessibility and the fine panorama seen from its summit. The ascent is an easy 1,200-foot scramble from the pass and the view extends from Mt. Williamson in the south to the Evolution and Abbot groups in the north. The

Muir Hut
(Photo by Norman Clyde, Eastern California Museum Collection)

sight of scores of peaks from the summit in winter, arrayed in splendid snowy garb, is grand almost beyond description.

Rae Lake possesses one of the most wildly picturesque settings of any in the Sierra, consisting of numerous rugged peaks, several of which exceed 13,000 feet in elevation. Of these Black and Diamond Peaks might be mentioned. Neither is difficult of ascent; neither has been climbed more than a few times and both overlook deep, narrow gorges and ragged ridges, composed largely of dark schists and slates, in which a few mountain sheep still linger, although they are seldom seen except when winter snows drive them far down the eastern slope of the Sierra toward Owens Valley. A few miles farther north is Baxter Peak. The view from the more easterly of its two peaks down the great eastern scarp of the Sierra, is very impressive.

A very interesting but seldom-visited portion of the Sierra is the upper basin of the south fork of the Kings River. It is largely above timberline, is some miles in extent and is surrounded by mountains, some of which are above 13,000 feet, and one — Split Mountain — over 14,000 feet. Excepting the latter, the most outstanding peak around the basin is Pinchot, 13,471 feet in elevation.

It is also the most conspicuous of a number of deeply-colored mountains of this part of the range, owing their reds and browns to slates and schists surviving from the sedimentary deposits that once covered the Sierra. Their warmth of hue is an agreeable change from the uniform gray tones that usually appear in the granite, which is the preponderating rock in the range.

Just to the north of Mt. Pinchot is Striped Mountain (13,160'), so named from the contorted bands of schist and quartzite which compose a large portion of its metamorphic mass. Interesting rock-work can be had up its steeper faces, but it is not what would be called a difficult mountain.

North of Striped Mountain, across Taboose Pass, is Cardinal Mountain (13,388'), deriving its name from a capping of cardinal schist and slate that forms a considerable portion of it and extends northward in a conspicuous layer along the crest of the arete that connects it with Split Mountain. The ascent is extremely easy and the view obtained is an excellent one, especially of the deep cirque to the north, across which frowns the great furrowed face of Split Mountain, banded with red, orange and black.

Although the main peaks of the Palisade group reach elevations greater than 13,500 feet, there are several lower ones that are extremely picturesque and which afford excellent climbing. The finest of these summits is Temple Crag (Mt. Alice), 13,016 feet in height. It is doubtful whether there is a more beautiful and striking "crag-mountain" in the Sierra Nevada. Its northern and northeastern faces are sheer precipices varied by numbers of spiry, turret-like, pinnacles beautifully placed.

The ascent is a thrilling, but not especially dangerous, rock-climb, and has been accomplished several times. The view at its summit is circumscribed, but as the crag stands near the center of the Palisade amphitheater it affords, perhaps, the best view to be had of this great cirque walled in to the south by the magnificent Palisades, whose dark serrated forms rise from a series of glaciers that cling to their bases and send icy fingers far up the steep chutes that furrow their northern fronts. To the west of Temple

Mt. Haeckel
(Photo by Norman Clyde, Eastern California Museum Collection)

Crag and connected with it by an impassable knife-edge is an unnamed pinnacle 13,400 feet in altitude, which commands a very fine view of the palisades and offers an interesting rock-climb up its northwestern face. It has probably been climbed but once.

In the Evolution Basin, a mountain-encircled oval depression some six or eight miles in length containing the headwaters of a tributary of the south fork of the San Joaquin, there are several peaks between 13,000 and 13,500 feet worthy of note. Looking southward across Evolution Lake, one is impressed by Mts. Spencer and Huxley, sharp, granite peaks, the latter 13,124 feet in height. Both stand well out toward the middle of the basin so that their summits command a very good panorama of the wild, craggy mountains that encircle them. Mt. Huxley is an excellent rock-climb that is not attended by any especial danger or difficulty.

Along the line of peaks bordering the basin to the east, is Mt. Haeckel (13,422′), a very beautiful peak tapering to a narrow

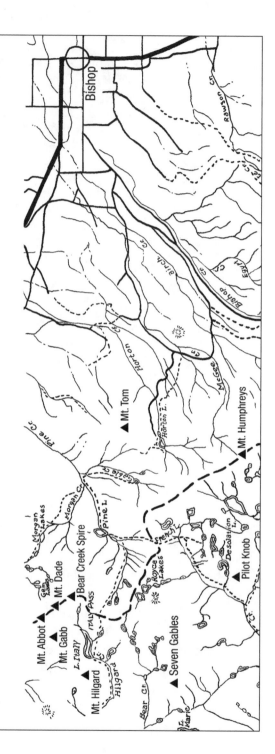

Peaks shown:

Mt. Sill
North Palisade
Mt. Winchell
Temple Crag
Agassiz Needle
Mt. Gilbert
Mt. Thompson
Mt. Powell
Mt. Haeckel
Mt. Wallace
Mt. Huxley
Mt. Goddard
Mt. McGee
The Hermit
Mt. Spencer
Mt. Darwin
Mt. Emerson
Mt. Humphreys
Mt. Tom
Pilot Knob
Seven Gables
Mt. Hilgard
Mt. Gabb
Mt. Abbot
Mt. Dade
Bear Creek Spire

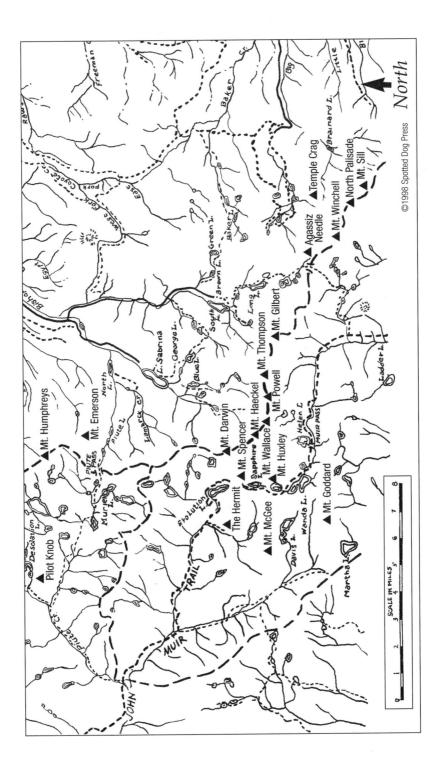

North

©1998 Spotted Dog Press

SCALE IN MILES

Mt. Humphreys

Mt. Emerson

Pilot Knob

Mt. Darwin

Mt. Spencer

Mt. Haeckel

Mt. Wallace

Mt. Huxley

Mt. Powell

Mt. Thompson

Mt. Gilbert

Agassiz Needle

Temple Crag

Mt. Winchell

North Palisade

Mt. Sill

The Hermit

Mt. McGee

Mt. Goddard

JOHN MUIR TRAIL

PIUTE PASS

MUIR PASS

Evolution L.

Helen L.

Wanda L.

Martha L.

Davis L.

Desolation L.

Mt. Sabrina

George L.

Blue L.

South Brown L.

Green L.

Baker L.

Long L.

Ladder L.

Brainard L.

Bishop Cr.

East Fork

West Fork

East Fork Coyote Cr.

North Coyote Cr.

Freeman Cr.

Rawson Cr.

Piute Cr.

Lamarck Cr.

North L.

Piute L.

Muriel L.

Baker Cr.

Little B.

Big B.

point — a fine example of what might be termed a Gothic type of peak, not uncommon in the Sierra Nevada. Nearby are other similar ones, including Mt. Wallace and several unnamed ones to the east. They are impressive, seen from Evolution Basin, but still more so, looking from the northeast up the amphitheater of the middle fork of Bishop Creek, as they form a beautiful and inspiring group of sharp peaks — snow-splashed in summer, snow-clad in winter — with Mt. Haeckel the outstanding member of the cluster. It is a fairly difficult climb that has been negotiated several times. To the northeast of the amphitheater are several flat-topped peaks somewhat above 13,000 feet in elevation. Among these are Mts. Gilbert, Thompson and Powell. They form a striking portion of an almost complete circle of mountains about the middle fork of Bishop Creek and have seldom been scaled.

When one nears Piute Pass from the east, he is flanked on either side by two fine peaks — Mt. Emerson to the right and an unnamed one to the left. The first can be climbed by following any one of a number of steep chutes that run up its southern face, and on its summit a good view is obtained, especially of Mt. Humphreys, which looms grandly across a cirque to the northwest. It is an imposing peak from an elevation to the south and southeast and displays more or less of a warm red hue that increases in depth in a long line of pinnacles that run eastward from it. Seen from the Piute trail, the other peak is both beautiful and striking. Probably neither peak has been climbed more than once.

Situated in a rather isolated position on the headwaters of Bear Creek and attaining an altitude of 13,066 feet is Seven Gables. It is a conspicuous mountain, from any direction, and on account of its position a wide view is obtained from its summit. Several miles northward from Seven Gables is Mt. Hilgard (13,361'), one of a circle of peaks that surround Italy Basin. It is easy of ascent and commands a good prospect far and near, overlooking the barren but attractive depression of Lake Italy Basin to the northeast; the interesting region of Bear Creek and the Vermillion Cliffs nearby to the northwest, while its more extensive panorama extends far up and down the range. Northward from Mt. Hilgard a few miles is Mt. Mills (13,353′), a peak that rises in very rugged surroundings, is an attractive climb, and has probably not been scaled more than once.

As one looks northward from the summit of any of the last-named peaks, he descries, not many miles distant, a group of softly-colored mountains whose reds and browns delight the eye, surmounted by one considerably higher, Red Slate Mountain, a readily climbed peak that overlooks a wide panorama. North of this group the Sierra drops down in a deep depression, to rise again in the Ritter and Lyell groups, belonging to the mountains of the Yosemite region, beyond the limits of the Southern Sierra.

The scenic character of a mountain, after all, and its spectacular aspects, depend more on the close juxtaposition of height and depression rather than upon mere elevation. There is little apparent difference between a precipice with a thousand-foot sheer declivity and one that falls away for fifteen hundred feet. Hence many of the most imposing of Sierra peaks will be found in the 13,000-13,500-foot group.

Beautiful blue,
partially covered with ice,
nestling among granite walls.
The pyramidal Sawtooth Peak
directly to the southwest.

Journal entry
Columbine Lake

12,000-FOOT PEAKS

Arrow Peak

R.D.

Compared with the great number of peaks in the southern Sierra ranging from 13,000 to 14,000 feet in elevation —upwards of a hundred and fifty — those that do not attain an altitude of 13,000 feet appear to be relatively low and sometimes almost insignificant, yet scattered along this portion of the range there are many fine peaks between 12,000 and 13,000 feet in height — peaks striking in appearance, difficult to scale and affording excellent views from their summits. On account of the great average elevation of the Kern region, they are perhaps fewest in this portion of the Sierra, yet even there are found some worthy of mention.

In the more southerly portion of the Great Western Divide are many peaks that afford interesting climbs and good views, especially of the Kaweahs, a beautiful cluster of peaks that dominates the Kern region to the west of the Kern River. Perhaps the best of these is Sawtooth Peak (12,340′). Its sharp pyramidal summit can be seen far down the western slope of the range and in clear winter weather can be identified from the San Joaquin Valley and perhaps even from the summit of the Coast Range. It forms a worthy introduction to the High Sierra for those entering the Sierra by way of Cliff Creek and over Black Rock Pass. Farther north on the same divide, northwest of the Kaweahs, is

Triple Divide Peak (12,651'), one that affords some rock-climbing, is a rather impressive pyramid-like peak and commands a fine panorama.

From its summit the view of the precipitous north face of the Kaweahs is superb, as is also the one along the jagged line of Kern-Kaweah Divide; of the sheer cliffs on the western front of some of them and of the cirques, often adorned with alpine tarns that appear far below. Very pleasing also is the sight of the dark undulating conifer forest, in which one can descry in the distance the Giant Forest, and far beyond it the hazy San Joaquin Valley.

On the opposite side of the range, overlooking Owens Valley is Lone Pine Peak, slightly under 13,000 feet in height. From the valley, on account of standing well out in the great eastern scarp, it is one of the most striking peaks in the vicinity, vying with con- siderably higher neighbors. It has probably not been ascended more than two or three times, although it can be scaled with com- parative ease from the headwaters of the south fork of Lone Pine Creek. The view from the summit is very fine, especially of Mt. Whitney and the eastern scarp of the Sierra, of which this peak possesses an unobstructed view northward for some fifty miles of the highest portion of the range.

In the Kings watershed noteworthy 12,000-foot peaks are more numerous. Perhaps the most beautiful of them is the East Vidette (12,742'). Seen from the north, especially from Vidette Meadow and the vicinity of Bullfrog Lake, there is perhaps no peak in the Sierra possessing more pleasing lines that converge from a broad base to a narrow summit, forming a symmetrical pyramid with a beautifully furrowed front. Its sober gray color is set off by a mantle of dark foxtail and tamarack pine that sweeps up from the meadow at its base to its precipitous walls. The ascent is a rock-climb of some difficulty that has been made about a dozen times. On account of its central position, the summit commands a magnificent view of the great jagged peaks that extend around the amphitheater in an almost complete circle.

On the divide between the Kings-Kern amphitheater and the

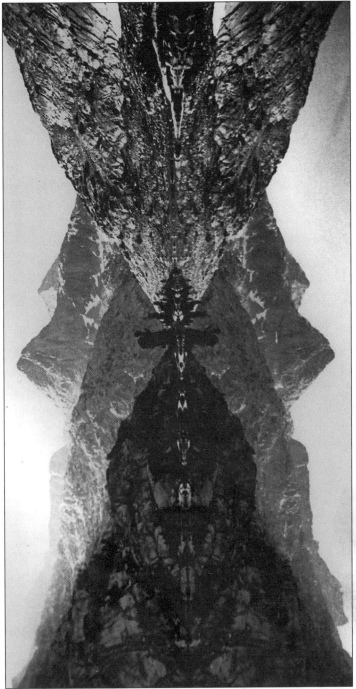

Mt. Spencer (Photo: Norman Clyde, Eastern California Museum Collection)

Rae Lake Basin are several peaks deserving of mention, notably Mt. Rixford (12,856') and Mt. Gardiner (12,903'). The ascent of the former entails some rock-work of a not very difficult nature, and the summit has an impressive view of the great amphitheater to the south and of Rae Lake basin to the north, with its chain of beautiful lakes. Farther west along the same ridge, jutting out northward from it is Mt. Gardiner. Possessing sheer cliffs to the west and north, it is an impressive peak from these directions. It can be ascended only from the south, and then by crossing a saddle from a slightly lower peak, working up a broken rock face for about a hundred feet and thence along a ragged knife-edge to the highest point about fifty yards distant. It is regarded as a difficult peak and has been scaled but few times.

One of the most sequestered basins of the High Sierra is Rae Lake Basin. It contains a chain of lakes of which Rae Lake, the largest, is also the finest, being indeed one of the most beautiful and picturesque in all the range. Ensconced in a deep bowl, rugged mountains rising on all sides, those to the south and southwest richly colored red, orange and black, bands of which run in a most bizarre fashion; varied by rocky islets and promontories sparsely clad with tamarack pines, it has become one of the favorites of those who frequent the Sierra.

One of the most fantastically banded of these mountains is Dragon Peak (12,955'), along the main crest of the range, to the northeast of the lake. It terminates in a sharp pinnacle which offers an interesting rock scramble that probably only two parties have made, and overlooks an extremely ragged and broken portion of the eastern escarpment of the Sierra.

A few miles to the northwest of the lake, from a basin dotted with alpine tarns called Sixty Lake Basin, rises a rather solitary mountain of the Matterhorn type, a beautiful pyramid from whatever angle it may be viewed and generally conceded to be one of the most difficult ascents of the Sierra.

This is Mt. King, 12,909 feet in elevation. All the ascents except one, have been accomplished by following a narrow shelf that runs diagonally up the almost vertical eastern face of the mountain to a point a few rods below the summit. From there the climber hoists himself over large rocks to a little alcove above a steep precipice and perhaps fifteen feet below the summit. Here he is confronted by a vertical "pitch." After groping around he finds a fingerhold and a cup-like depression that forms a tolerably safe foothold. Swinging himself up he grasps the top of the rock above, conscious that the precipice awaits him if he should let go. Reaching the former safely he encounters a weather-polished rounded boulder over which he can reach a short distance.

Up this he scrambles and finds himself on the summit only a few feet in diameter. In three directions ragged knife-edges drop away; in two there are almost vertical precipices, while in the third it slopes down at a very steep angle. As it stands comparatively alone it possesses a much finer view than would be expected from its height. To the west it looks down into Paradise Valley, one of the most beautiful gorges in the Sierra; to the northeast by Mt. Pinchot, other nearby highly colored peaks are conspicuous, as are also the Palisades farther to the north and Mt. Goddard to the northwest; to the south the serrated line of the Kings-Kern Divide looms high across the intervening ridge. In the descent one can drop from shelf to shelf down the eastern face of the mountain for twenty or thirty feet until he strikes the other route. Mt. King is what mountaineers sometimes term a "tow-man" mountain – one which contains pitches that are difficult for a single mountaineer to surmount but may sometimes be negotiated without great trouble by a party of two or more by reason of mutual assistance. About ten have stood on the summit of Mt. King.

From Woods Lakes, a delightful group near Sawmill Pass, one can climb Colosseum Mountain (12,417'), an easy ascent that possesses a good view. A short distance northward along the crest is Mt. Perkins (12,557'), which has some rock-climbing and has probably been climbed but once. A charming camping place a few miles to the northwest is Bench Lake. As its name implies,

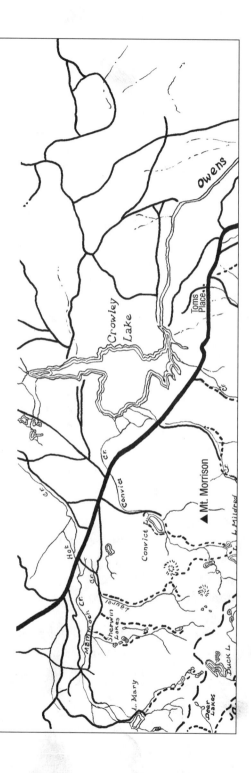

Peaks shown:

Mt. Hilgard
Mt. Gabb
Bear Creek Spire
Mt. Dade
Mt. Abbot
Mt. Mills
Mt. Morgan
Red and
  White Mtn.
Mt. Morrison

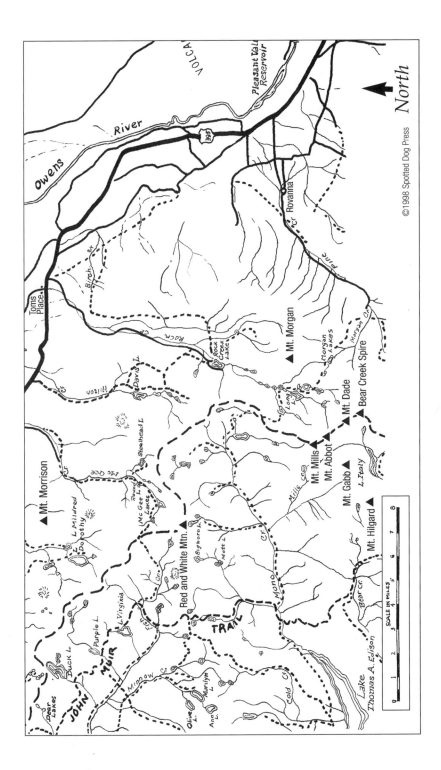

it is situated on a bench overlooking the south fork of the Kings River only a few miles from its source. The rocky terrain to the north and the long promontories that jut out into the usually placid water of the lake and several rock islets are clothed with a scattered growth of tamarack pines, while to the southwest rises a beautiful peak called Arrow Mountain, with symmetrical pyramidal form. From the lake it can be ascended with comparative ease and the climber is rewarded with a magnificent view.

Passing northwestward to the Evolution group, one finds there also several interesting 12,000-foot peaks. North from Mt. Goddard is a dark, picturesque, but somewhat forbidding peak — Mt. McGee, 12,966 feet in height; a rather difficult climb commanding an excellent view, especially down into Goddard Canyon, a beautiful tributary to the south fork of the San Joaquin River. Probably it has been climbed but twice. Northward several miles from it is The Hermit (12,352'). Viewed from Colby Meadows to the northwest, it ranks among the most beautiful mountains in the Sierra. Its slender gray cone rises from a verdant meadow and a grove of tamarack pines, and is especially striking when clouds hang about its narrow summit. The ascent is a rock climb of some difficulty, as the latter consists of a rounded monolith which is troublesome for a single mountaineer to surmount, as it is without holds and is higher than one can reach. It has been climbed several times.

Entering Evolution Basin from the north, ones attention is attracted by two striking peaks that rise picturesquely to the south beyond the curving expanse of Evolution Lake. They are Mts. Spencer and Huxley. The former is easily climbed and is a very good vantage point from which to view the mountains around the Evolution Basin.

As one follows the trail up Piute Creek, a sharp pinnacle appears to block the way. It is very striking, especially in the evening when sunset colors gild its granite shaft. It is called Pilot Knob (12,227') and although sheer to the west, it can be easily climbed from the east, and is an excellent point from which to survey the surrounding higher mountains, especially Mt. Humphreys, towering to the east across an undulating timberless basin.

One of the most beautiful of the lakes to the east of the Sierra crest is Convict Lake. On three sides of it rise picturesque mountains, the most imposing of which is Mt. Morrison, whose bold, sheer summit, 12,245 feet in elevation, rises to the south of the lake. Although obviously unscaleable from the east, it probably can be ascended from the opposite direction. Along with most of the peaks of this group. It is remarkable for its richness of coloring — the red of the slate predominating amid the gray of quartzite and the black of schist.

A few miles to the west is Red and White Mountain, reported to be rather difficult of ascent. The majority found in this area are easy to climb, except that sometimes one encounters wearisome slopes of disintegrated slate. They form the northern terminus of the Southern Sierra. From them one looks northward and northwestward to the dark cluster consisting of Mts. Ritter, Banner and the Minarets; to the snowy summits of the Lyell group and the undulating skyline of those to the south and east of the headwaters of the Merced River.

The above sketchings may give those unacquainted with the Sierra Nevada some slight idea of the beauty and grandeur of the highest peaks in this lofty and magnificent range. However, it is only by climbing them that one can acquire a full appreciation of them. Even repeated ascents continually reveal something new, as no mountains are altogether the same on any two occasions. Of all of the ranges in the United States there is probably none that offers such opportunity for strenuous but healthful mountain climbing as does the Sierra Nevada.

The falls are unusually full for the season,
the never ending fascination of the Yosemite.
I believe the falls are fuller than
I have ever seen before.
Numerous transient falls with cascades
on both sides of the valley.
Vernal and Nevada showing their
particular types of beauty, more than
I have ever seen before;
the cascades bounding more gloriously.

Journal entry
Yosemite

PEAKS OF THE YOSEMITE REGION

Mts. Lyell & McClure

Although neither so high, so rugged nor so picturesque as the mountains of the southern Sierra, those of the Yosemite possess fascinating scenery and a considerable number of peaks sufficiently difficult to attract the attention of the climber.

As one looks northward from almost any of the loftier eminences of the southern Sierra, his attention is always focused for a time on a dark, striking group consisting of Mts. Ritter, Banner and the Minarets situated between the headwaters of the north and the middle forks of the San Joaquin River, just outside of the boundary of the Yosemite National Park.

With the possible exception of the Mt. Lyell group they are the most impressive group of the region and are undoubtedly the most ruggedly alpine. Forming a somewhat isolated group, they are readily distinguished for great distances from several directions, especially from the axis of the Sierra and from the crest of the desert ranges to the east, while from a large portion of Mono County they are conspicuous as they rise in a spectacular fashion beyond the forested area of the Mammoth Lakes region.

Mt. Ritter attains an elevation of 13,156 feet above sea-level, is the highest mountain north of the southern Sierra in the Sierra Nevada proper, is generally regarded as the most difficult of the loftier mountains of the Yosemite region, and possesses one of the finest views in this part of the range. While not an unusually difficult mountain, it requires caution on the part of the amateur and even experienced mountaineers have at times failed to reach its summit. Although it has been climbed from the east, the routes usually followed are from the west and the north. There seems, however, to be some difficulty in following the former, as several parties have unwittingly gotten off it and missed their objective. Nor is it the most accessible side of the mountain. The best route appears to be one up the north face of the peak, that can be approached from either the northwest or the northeast by swinging around the west or the east shoulder of Mt. Banner just north of Mt. Ritter.

Arriving on the saddle between the two mountains, one follows a broad chute midway up the steep face to a point several hundred feet below the summit, where he swings to the left up a narrow shelf that reaches the crest about fifty yards east of the summit, to which he can easily walk. During summer months which have an unusual amount of snow, some difficulty might be encountered on this route. The panorama seen from the summit extends far over the desert mountains and valleys to the east. The immediate surroundings are extremely alpine, being composed of craggy mountains and deep gorges.

Running south from Mt. Ritter is a long line of dark pinnacles called the Minarets. The highest of these has been scaled but once and is considered one of the most difficult rockclimbs of the Sierra. To the north of Mt. Ritter — so close as to be a twin peak — is Mt. Banner, a peak with a precipitous northern slope, but a gentle and easily scaled southern one. It stands out in a very spectacular fashion from Garnet and Thousand Island lakes. The latter is an ultramarine tarn lying in the shadow of the jagged Minarets. Handsome mountain hemlocks dot the northern slopes, while from the south and the west great chunks of snow and ice drop into its deep blue water where they float for days before they eventually melt. Other nearby interesting phenomena are the Devil's Postpile, a striking mass of basaltic columns a few

Mt. Lyell from the summit of Mt. McClure (Photo by Pete Yamagata)

miles to the southeast, and Rainbow Falls, a snow-white cataract plunging over dark lava rock, several miles to the south.

Looking northwestward from the summit of Mt. Ritter one sees a group of mountains of which the highest is Mt. Lyell (13,090'). It possesses the largest glacier in the Sierra Nevada and is undoubtedly the most beautiful mountain in the Yosemite region. In composition and perspective, as one views its glacier-mantled north flank rising abruptly at the head of Lyell Creek, it has appealed to many artists. The ascent is usually effected from the north across the glacier and up a chimney or over a rocky comb to the dark, granite summit that projects above the glacier. It is usually of only ordinary difficulty except late in the season. The glacier is sometimes covered with snow hummocks several feet in height that render progress difficult.

The view from the top is one of the finest in this part of the range. To the southeast it commands the Ritter group; to the south it looks down upon the upper cirque and canyon and

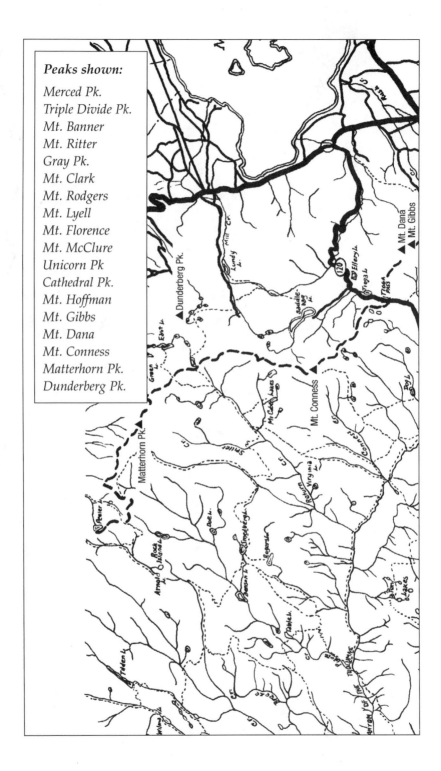

Peaks shown:

Merced Pk.
Triple Divide Pk.
Mt. Banner
Mt. Ritter
Gray Pk.
Mt. Clark
Mt. Rodgers
Mt. Lyell
Mt. Florence
Mt. McClure
Unicorn Pk
Cathedral Pk.
Mt. Hoffman
Mt. Gibbs
Mt. Dana
Mt. Conness
Matterhorn Pk.
Dunderberg Pk.

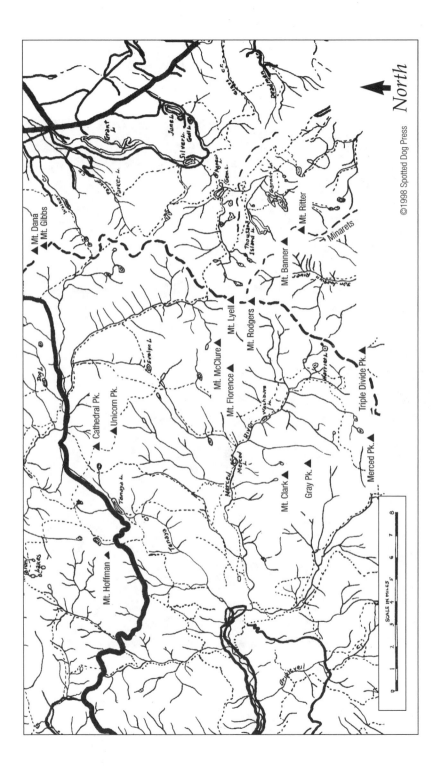

North

© 1998 Spotted Dog Press

Clyde relaxing
(Photo by Cedric Wright, The Colby Library, Sierra Club)

across them to the Merced peaks and far beyond them to the massed peaks of the southern Sierra; to the north and the northwest, down into the wide alpine basin of Tuolumne Meadow and across it to Mt. Conness and a score of rugged peaks in the northwestern portion of the park. Mt. McClure, to the west of Mt. Lyell can readily be climbed from the saddle between the two mountains. To the east of Mt. Lyell, across the Merced cirque is Mt. Rodgers, another 13,000-foot-peak worthy of an ascent.

From the top of Mt. Lyell, in a northeasterly direction one sees a group of mountains, differing from the usual sharply-cut granite peaks typical of the Sierra, in their rounded outlines and warmer colors, various hues of red, touched with a shade of light green from lichens and mineral stain. The most outstanding of these is Mt. Dana (13,050'). It can readily be climbed from the vicinity of Tioga Pass, the ascent being little more than a trudge up a steep slope of slate occurring in low shelves, angular rocks, and toward the summit, of loose scree. It overlooks the steep eastern scarp of the Sierra — here about 7,500 feet — across the circular, gray-green expanse of Mono Lake, eastward over range after range of desert mountains; southward past the Ritter group to the southern Sierra; northwestward along the ragged peaks along the northern border of the park.

Being at the head of Tuolumne Meadow it possesses a very fine prospect down this oval basin some ten miles in length, the Tuolumne River winding sinuously through verdant meadows that rise gently to deep green belts of conifer forest which sweep up to the gray snow-splashed peaks forming the skyline on either side of it.

Somewhat more than half way down the meadow and to the south of it is a cluster of unusually sharp peaks that shoot up abruptly from pine clad slopes. They rise in isolated spires and ragged ridges that have been termed "cockscombs." The best known of these are the Unicorn and Cathedral peaks. Both are somewhat difficult ascents; the former demanding some rather delicate rock-work along a broken knife-edge, to reach the summit, a narrow rock 10,849 feet above sea-level. The latter involves a steep scramble that terminates in a twenty-foot climb up a vertical monolith that rises from a shelving alcove which pitches over a precipice. Two parallel cracks, several feet apart, extend up its face, and into these the climber thrusts hands and feet, working up to the summit, a platform a few feet in diameter and 10,933 feet above sea-level. Persons wearing rubber-soled shoes may spiral around the final rock in a slightly different course. Both have excellent views of the northern half of the park.

North of the lower portion of Tuolumne Meadow is a handsome, light gray mountain that from many points to the south stands in fine perspective at the head of receding canyons. This is Mt. Conness (12,556'). The ascent is comparatively easy, varied by several hundred feet of steep climbing just below the summit, which drops away in vertical crags to the southwest and breaks rapidly down to a small glacier on the north. It commands an extensive view, especially of the series of rough peaks that run westward from it, forming the northern boundary of the park and a large area of the lower but interesting mountains to the north of the park.

The trail north of the Tuolumne River leaps in snowy cascades and whirling water-wheel falls for a distance of eighteen miles until it is eventually ensconced in a great steep canyon with walls a mile high. A number of canyons are crossed and can be followed up to their terminuses at the base of the peaks along the northern boundary of the park, to Dunderberg Peak, a dark slate mountain, with a good view. Another enticing option is Matterhorn Canyon which can be reached through groves of exquisite mountain hemlocks, where insects have not killed them, and on to the Matterhorn which offers an excellent, but not very difficult rock climb, to its narrow summit overlooking a fine panorama that extends far along the axis of the range — south to the southern Sierra, north over undulating mountains that rise again in the mountains around Lake Tahoe. Directly to the west of the Matterhorn is a fine line of granite sawtooths. Along the

Climbers on Cathedral Peak, Eichorn Pinnacle in background
(Photo by Pete Yamagata)

main trail, a few miles farther west, around Rodgers Lake, an extremely beautiful lake, are several peaks that are worthy of a scramble to their summits while along the northwestern limit of the park is Tower Peak (11,702'), a rather isolated mountain that affords both a good climb and an extensive view.

Returning to the lower portion of Tuolumne Meadow and looking southwest one sees Mt. Hoffman, an apparently flat-topped mountain not of great height but situated in a central and somewhat isolated position that causes it to command one of the best views to be had of Yosemite Park in its length and breadth. It was one of the favorite mountains of John Muir. The ascent can be easily made from the Tioga Road that passes several miles to the south. Just north of the peak is Nine Lake Basin, containing a con-siderable number of beautiful tarns counter-sunk, as it were, in a rocky terrain and overhung by groves of graceful mountain hem-locks. Nearby them to the north are several points from which one looks down into the Grand Canyon of the Tuolumne River.

As one looks eastward from almost any of the numerous vantage points that rise on either side of the Yosemite Valley, he is impressed by a number of fine peaks that shut in the upper Merced Valley to the south. Striking in summer, they are more so in winter when their craggy peaks rise from undulating plateaus and deep basins covered by a stainless robe of snow. The most imposing of these is Mt. Clark. Its bold, sharp peak, of the Matterhorn type, rises so abruptly as to render it much more spectacular than would be expected from its actual height, which is only 11,506 feet. Although it can be climbed up the steeply shelving western face, the usual route followed is from the north which is an easy one except for a few rods of rather eerie knife-edge just below the top which is only a few feet in diameter. This peak, whose rock structure indicates that it was originally a dome, has been attacked on three sides by glaciers that have carved it into a typical Matterhorn with three aretes running out from a narrow summit. It is the best example of this type of mountain to be found in the Yosemite. The panorama seen is especially fine, extending to the distant south along the higher portion of the Sierra that rises majestically in the distance across a great depression.

Running eastward from Mt. Clark are Gray, Merced and Triple Divide peaks, all readily scaleable from the upper Merced. The views from all are excellent, that from Triple Divide Peak being perhaps the most noteworthy, as it stands between the watersheds of the Merced, both the main and the south forks, and a tributary of the San Joaquin. It is a slate mountain as are also one or two of its neighbors to the west. Mt. Florence to the east of Merced Lake can be climbed from it as a starting point. The upper Merced Canyon and amphitheater is an interesting region. In addition to its beautiful mountains are the fine cascades and apron-falls of its higher reaches, and the emerald green Merced meandering through groves of tamarack pine and quaking aspen above Washburn Lake.

Although surpassed by the southern Sierra in loftiness and ruggedness, the Yosemite region is superior to it in waterfalls and cascades and in addition contains the Yosemite Valley. As a whole, although not as epic in grandeur as the southern portion of the range, it is a fascinating region with few equals.

Norman Clyde demonstrating a dulfersitz.
(Photographer unknown, The Bancroft Library)

THREE SUPERLATIVES IN THE SEQUOIA

Within the limits of Sequoia National Park, California, is the tallest mountain in the continental United States, the highest altitude lake of its or greater magnitude, and the largest and oldest tree in the world.

Mt. Whitney, situated on the main crest of the Sierra Nevada, attains an elevation of 14, 496 feet above sea level, the highest of a number of peaks in the southern portion of the Sierra Nevada, almost rivaling it in altitude. To the northeast only a few miles distant past the shoulder of Mt. Russell, 14,086 feet in height, one standing on the summit of Mt. Whitney, catches a glimpse of Tulainyo Lake, lying on the very crest of the Sierra at an elevation of 12,865 feet above sea level. Its cobalt blue waters extend in an oval form approximately a half mile in length and are without a visible outlet. On account of its great altitude and the shadows cast by the surrounding peaks, it is often not entirely free from ice until late summer.

Upwards of fifty miles west of Mt. Whitney but concealed from one on its summit by the intervening Great Western Divide, a line of jagged peaks of which some are almost 14,000 feet in altitude, lies the Giant Forest, containing the largest and oldest of living things. A number of other groves of Sequoia gigantea, the Sierra Sequoia, are found for a distance of somewhat over a hundred miles on the western slope of the Sierra — notably the Tuolumne and the Mariposa in the Yosemite Park and General Grant National Park — but none contains so many trees or occupies so great an area as does Giant Forest. To it also belongs the honor of having the largest of the sequoias — the General Sherman, a colossal tree with an average basal diameter of 32.7 feet, a height of 272.4 feet, and a volume of 49,770 cubic feet. Its age is estimated between three and four thousand years.

Greatly imposing view of the serrated,
glacier-sculptured wall of the
Great Western Divide. Beyond it, the Kaweahs
obscured by shifting mass of cloud.
Fascinating camp among the red firs
surrounded by meadow. Meadow flowers along
the trail to the Kaweahs.
The firs standing with dark silhouetted forms
in the light of the full moon.
The high mountain crests showing roseate
in the light of the setting sun,
then fading to gray, then glimmering obscurely
in the moonlight.
Flowers, flowers almost everywhere.

Journal entry
From Alta Peak

FROM THE TALLEST TREES TO THE HIGHEST MOUNTAIN

One of the most remarkable trails in the United States is the recently constructed one beginning at Crescent Meadow in the heart of the Giant Forest and terminating on the summit of Mt. Whitney, the highest point on the crest of the Sierra Nevada. The diversity of the scenery which it traverses is nothing short of marvelous. The greatest trees in the world, at least one of its most beautiful canyons, and the loftiest mountain in the continental United States are indeed the major, but only a few of the many scenic attractions along the High Sierra Trail. The High Sierra Trail, some seventy-miles long, contours along granite cliffs, climbs high passes and descends into deep canyons on its varied course.

Not only is this trail of great value because of the superlative scenery within view from it, but also because it intersects most of the other trails of the great mountain hinterland of the Sequoia National Park in such a way that almost any place in it accessible by trail can be reached without difficulty, merely by leaving the "trunk" trail, as it were, and proceeding north or south from it. This enables one "to circle" around almost at will in the great "backcountry" of the park.

Leaving the end of the paved road at Crescent Meadow, the finest and most extensive stand of Sequoias in the Sierra Nevada, the High Sierra Trail strikes eastward on a gently rising gradient, at first beneath the shade of great conifers, but presently deserting these to swing out along the open face of a mountain slope falling away several thousand feet into the broad, deep basin of the Middle Fork of the Kaweah River. Southward, paralleling this runs a forest-clad ridge with an even skyline except where broken by the granite domes and spires of Cathedral Rocks. To the east, forming a great barrier at the head of the canyon, extends the serrated line of the peaks of the Great Western Divide, with

Steve Wyckoff, Dot Leavitt and Ansel Adams in the commissary
at Crabtree Camp on one of Clyde's Sierra Club High Trips.
(Photo by W.L. Huber, The Bancroft Library)

several of the Kaweahs almost 14,000 feet in elevation towering
beyond them.

For miles, the trail advances almost directly eastward in a
course in places undulating, but with no steep gradients as it contours around projecting ridges, withdraws into shaded recesses,
and crosses numerous ravines. Now it winds along through
magnificent stands of White Fir, Sugar Pine, and later, of Red Fir,
then traverses sunny slopes or swings along beneath the shade of
deciduous oaks, and occasionally cuts directly through an inter-
cepting mass of granite. About ten miles from the Giant Forest,
an old trail is passed leading down to Redwood Meadow from
which Black Rock and several other passes of the more southerly
portion of the Great Western Divide can be reached.

After dipping down into Buck Canyon, fourteen miles from Giant Forest, the trail taking a southeasterly course, climbs a ridge densely clad with fir, crosses its summit, and continues eastward through Bearpaw Meadow, once a favorite of John Muir on account of its lavish wealth of flowers. Near it, a branch trail descends southward to River Valley, as the upper portion of the valley of the Middle Fork is called. The scenery rapidly becomes more spectacular. Sheer granite crags drop away to the floor of River Valley. Eastward beyond the latter, granite cliffs sweep up into domes and minarets above which in turn are the hollow cirques and sharp peaks of the Great Western Divide.

After rounding several beetling crags, the trail swerves to the left and crosses the Upper Kaweah River. Southeast across Hamilton Creek, one obtains superb views of granite domes and spires. Here, a trail diverges to the north by which one can reach Tamarack Lake — nestling on the floor of a fine cirque and said to harbor trout of monstrous size, or one can cross Elizabeth Pass and descend into the watershed of the South Fork of the Kings River.

East of the stream the trail switchbacks up an abrupt mountain slope for a few hundred feet, rounds a point commanding an excellent view of the forested canyon of River Valley running in a southeasterly direction, and after a short descent, proceeds eastward along the face of a granite cliff in which a way has been blasted for it. With this behind, it crosses Hamilton Creek and proceeds upstream switchbacking over several step-like rises. Presently, at an elevation of slightly over 8,000 feet, it veers to the left on a level with Hamilton Lake. This is one of the choicest spots in the Sierra. Around a sapphire lake rises a mountain amphitheater culminating in striking and pleasingly colored peaks, spires, turrets and domes. North of the lake, granite cliffs rise sheer for some 2,000 feet in a great fluted wall surmounted by sharp spires – the Angel's Wing, it has been called.

From Hamilton Lake, the trail zigzags up a precipitous mountainside to the north. The blue lake on the floor of the amphitheater and the peaks crowning its great, ruggedly sculptured wall, notably Mt. Stewart to the north and Eagle Scout Peak to the south of Kaweah Gap, toward which the trail steadily climbs, affording one a continuous succession of inspiring views. After ascending for a vertical distance of some 1,500 feet, and a horizontal distance of about another mile, the trail then swings abruptly around a point, within view of a steel suspension bridge spanning a deep gorge. A hundred and twenty-five feet in length, it is the second largest bridge of its kind in the national parks of the United States. The material of which it is composed, twenty-two tons in amount, was packed in on muleback for some eighteen miles.

Beyond the bridge, the trail ascends gradually as it continues southwestward through meadows in mid-summer, gay with numerous varieties of alpine flowers, among others, the leopard lilly, senecio, columbine, larkspur, and Pride of the Sierra. At an altitude of about 10,000 feet it passes to the left of a small lake and begins to switchback eastward toward Kaweah Gap, then a little over a mile distant. Presently, one comes within view of a lake of cobalt blue nestling beneath precipices displaying a pleasingly mottled effect of blended gray, black, red, green and brown. Southward beyond the crags immediately above the lake rises the sheer north face of Eagle Scout Peak. The ultramarine blue lake with its extremely rugged setting forms one of the scenic gems of the Sierra.

Above the lake the trail continues past several lakelets and through a succession of small meadows bright with red heather, kalmia and wild cyclamen, and up a short series of switchbacks to Kaweah Gap, a notch in the Great Western Divide, some 10,800 feet above sea-level. Eastward the pass slopes away to Nine Lakes Basin, the headwaters of the Big Arroyo, beyond which rises steeply a shoulder of the Black Kaweah, 13, 752 feet in elevation, the most westerly of this very striking group of peaks. To the left, one looks northeastward across Nine Lakes Basin to Milestone and other high mountains on the northern portion of the Great Western Divide. To the southeast, one looks far down the Big Arroyo, over several miles of meadows and then over a shallow, forested canyon to where it narrows to a gorge, as it nears the great canyon of the Kern River.

After descending from the pass and traversing the meadows, a stand of lodgepole pine is entered. Near a log cabin about a hundred yards to the right of the trail nearly a mile beyond where it enters the forest, a cutoff goes southeastward to Little Five Lakes Basin, several miles distant, on the way to Black Rock Pass. An older trail heading to the same destination is passed somewhat farther down. The Little Five Lakes Basin commands a superb view of the spectacular Kaweah Peaks a few miles northward across the Big Arroyo. Also in its vicinity are many interesting and beautiful lakes and mountains.

A few miles farther down, the trail leaves the Big Arroyo by its steep north side and continues eastward across the Chagoopa Plateau, an extensive and comparatively level area averaging about 9,500 feet above sea level, and with the exception of a few meadows, clothed with an open stand of foxtail and lodgepole pines growing from a gravelly soil composed of disintegrated granite. Several miles of trail through this forest brings one to Moraine Lake at an altitude of almost 9,500 feet, a circular body of water a few hundred yards in diameter, surrounded with lodgepole pine and without a visible outlet, the water apparently seeping away through the porous formation underneath. To the north and in plain view, Mt. Kaweah, the loftiest of the group slopes upward to an elevation of 13,816 feet above sea level. During mornings and evenings, its red coloration and gently rounded contours are frequently reflected in the placid water of the solitary lake. The timber encircled margin of this lone sheet of water together with the form and color of Mt. Kaweah remind one strongly of the lakes and mountains of certain portions of the Rockies. A languorous atmosphere about the lake, uncommon at such an altitude, renders it a delightful spot at which to linger for several days, particularly as a resting place during a strenuous trip.

East of Moraine Lake, the trail winds through open forest past Sky Parlor Meadow for several miles and then begins to switchback downward, two or three miles of descent, bringing one to the floor of the canyon of the Kern River. After a sojourn in the high Sierra, few places are so delightful as the canyon of the Kern, with an elevation above sea-level ranging from 6,000 to 8,000 feet, and with granite walls rising abruptly for several thousand feet above the floor of the great gorge, thirty miles in length, displaying beautiful gradations and mottlings in gray, buff, red and even green, the richest and most varied in coloring of the great canyons of the Sierra. Its superb river now dashing and foaming in snowy cascades, now leisurely flowing in placid stretches and deep pools of emerald-hued water beneath overarching groves of cottonwood and avenues of pine and fir, it is indeed a mountain paradise in the heart of the loftiest portion of the Sierra Nevada.

In the canyon of the Kern River, one can go either north or south along a trail traversing its entire length. Southward it leads to Camp Lewis at its lower end. In going to Mt. Whitney by the nearest route, however, one continues upstream about eight miles to Junction Meadow at an elevation of 8,000 feet. The High Sierra Trail may eventually, however, cross from Nine Lakes Basin to the headwaters of the Kern-Kaweah and follow that stream down to the Kern. Junction Meadow is well-named. From it one can go westward up the Kern-Kaweah and swing northwestward over Colby Pass and continue to Roaring River onto the South Fork of the Kings River drainage; northward to the headwaters of the Kern River; northeastward toward Tyndall Creek; southeastward up a recently constructed portion of the High Sierra Trail to the Muir Trail and thence to Mt. Whitney. The name is probably due to the fact that the Kern-Kaweah River and Tyndall Creek flow into the Kern in the vicinity of the meadow.

The High Sierra Trail gradually climbs out of the canyon, affording many excellent views down its length and westward across it to the Kaweahs. Within a few miles, one crosses the east to the rim of the gorge, and is again in the High Sierra on an extensive undulating plateau-like area ranging from 10,000 to

Sequoia backcountry
(Photo by Cedric Wright, The Bancroft Library)

11,000 feet above sea-level and clothed in great part with an open growth of foxtail and lodgepole pines. A few miles of traveling through this elevated expanse brings one to Crabtree Meadow, the usual starting point for ascents of Mt. Whitney from the west. One may camp here, but since this meadow is about four miles from the actual base of the mountain and there are at least equally good camping spots nearer to it, one might as well continue some distance farther. In fact, a cutoff trail will probably be built from the north, intersecting the present one at a point a mile or two nearer to Mt. Whitney.

On the morning of a contemplated ascent of Mt. Whitney, whether afoot or on horseback, an early start should be made, as the distance to be traveled by trail to the top of the peak and return is upwards of eighteen miles and the virtual ascent involved is one of about 4,000 feet. An early arrival at the summit may also enable one to avoid afternoon electric storms which sometimes occur on it, especially during mid-summer.

From Crabtree Meadow, or thereabouts, the trail follows the course of the stream through meadows dotted with alpine flowers and open pine groves to an elevation of some 12,000 feet. Those afoot may here proceed eastward to the base of a large chute which they can climb and continue northeastward from its head, across the gently rising upper portion of the mountain to its summit. The trail, however, after rising gradually as it proceeds in a southeasterly direction for upwards of a mile, begins to switchback directly upward toward Mt. Whitney Pass. Just below the latter, at an elevation of about 13,500 feet above sea-level, it meets the trail, from over the pass. Here, during the building of the trail, a camp stood for several months — the highest of the trail construction camps of the Sierra.

At the junction of the trail, or rather the combined trails, swing abruptly northward toward the summit of Mt. Whitney, then about two miles distant. In passing along the upper reaches of the trail one should not fail to observe the vivid blue clumps of alpine polemonium, and the pink and white clusters of mountain phlox. Nowhere are these flowers finer than on Mt. Whitney, and the former sometimes even survives at the extreme altitude of 14,000 feet. After an ascent of several hundred feet by switchback, the trail swings around a shoulder and passes along the base of Mt. Muir 14,025 feet in elevation, the highest of the pinnacles along the crest extending southward from the summit of Mt. Whitney. For those fond of climbing, it affords a short but interesting scramble and an excellent view from its narrow, almost needle-like summit. Pinnacle after pinnacle is left behind as the trail advances, sometimes climbing or descending rather steep but short pitches in order to get around some especially stubborn buttress; sometimes contouring along; in general, steadily rising. The views obtained are superb — broad and panoramic, spanning across the great mountain-encircled Kern amphitheater from west to north; glimpses through notches between sharp peaks far down the precipitous eastern escarpment of the Sierra Nevada to the great basin of the Owens Valley, and far eastward over it across range after range of desert mountains.

Having passed the long line of pinnacles, the trail slowly ascends to the base of the last five hundred foot pitch. There it swerves to the left and in a short series of wide switchbacks attains the broad summit of the mountain rising at a gentle gradient northeastward to its highest point. Advancing directly toward it, the trail presently reaches the Smithsonian cabin, terminating within a few rods of the stone monument erected on the highest rock, 14,496 feet above sea-level.

The panoramic view obtained from the summit of Mt. Whitney is one of astonishing scope and diversity. On clear days, especially during early summer, the eye can follow the crest of the Sierra fifty miles northward to the lofty, jagged Palisades, and then slightly westward another fifty or more miles to the mountains of the Yosemite National Park. Eastward across successive ranges of arid mountains, one may perhaps at times descry the Charleston Mountains, the highest in Nevada. Southeastward, one gazes across seventy-five miles of desert to the Panamint

Range, bounding Death Valley to the west. One cannot see the
floor of this valley from the top of Mt. Whitney unless he possesses optics capable of looking over a range of mountains and
down into the depression beyond — or an over-active imagina-
tion, which amounts to the same thing. Southward, on occasion,
far across the Mojave Desert, both the San Bernadino and Sierra
Madre ranges are faintly visible; southwestward across the forested, undulating region of the lower Kern, Frazier Mountain and
others in the vicinity loom, enveloped in a violet haze. Westward,
the view is limited by the Great Western Divide, but through its
notches, perhaps glimpses may at times be obtained of the even-
topped crest of the Coast Range. The Divide likewise cuts off
most of the west slope of the Sierra beyond it, but the entire upper
basin of the Kern, encircled with lofty mountains, lies outspread
sweeping around from the southwest to the north.

Eleven other peaks attaining elevations over 14,000 feet —
ten in the Sierra, one in the White Mountains — are within sight
from the top of Whitney. Interesting also, is the great escarpment
of the Sierra, the greatest in the United States — fifty miles of
which can be seen from this lofty vantage point. The average vertical distance from the floor of the valley east of this portion of the
Sierra to the higher summits on its crest is about 9,000 feet. In the
case of Mt. Whitney, it is almost 11,000 feet.

The summit of Mt. Whitney gained, one may return to Giant
Forest by a diversity of routes, should he not wish to retrace his
way along the most direct one. Swinging southward along the
Muir Trail, he may continue south and southwestward until
Camp Lewis is reached at the lower end of the Kern Canyon.
From there he can cross the Great Western Divide by availing
himself of a trail leading to Farewell Gap, or by following the
Kern upstream a few miles, encounter trails ascending to several
passes between the latter and Kaweah Gap. The more southerly
of these bring one out in the vicinity of Mineral King; the more
northerly, at Redwood Meadow from which the High Sierra Trail
and Giant Forest can be easily regained. If he goes northward

along the Muir Trail within the limits of the park, he will eventually return to Junction Meadow, from which it is possible, not easily feasible — to follow a trail leading up to the Kern-Kaweah for several miles and then diverge northwestward from it over Colby Pass and down Roaring River to its junction with Deadman Creek, and from there southward over Elizabeth Pass and down the headwaters of the Middle Fork of the Kaweah to the High Sierra Trail.

A hurried trip may be made from the Giant Forest with a return in nine days, camps being made at Hamilton Lake, the Kern Canyon and Crabtree Meadow or vicinity. However, the scenery of the region traversed is so magnificent and varied that only in the case of urgent necessity should an attempt be made to complete the trip in so short a time.

An Evening Climb of Mt. Muir

It was nearing the end of a perfect day as I sauntered up the Mt. Whitney Trail from a 13,500 foot camp toward the summit of the mountain. The sun was swinging downward toward the long, serrated rampart of the Great Western Divide some distance north of the castellated group of the Kaweahs. From both, violet shadows had extended down over their cirque-carved flanks and were slowly stealing across the broad amphitheater of the head-waters of the Kern River toward the mountain on the main crest of the range.

Coming abreast of Mt. Muir, a 14,025 foot peak in the line of pinnacles extending southward from Mt. Whitney, partly for the sake of the short but rather strenuous climb up its steep western face to the narrow summit, and partly because of the excellent view afforded by the latter, I scrambled up to its narrow summit. To the eastward, the great eastern escarpment of the Sierra, a gorge-furrowed mountain wall almost two miles high, was already in shadow as was also the broad valley of the Owens River at its base. Up the slope of the Inyo Mountains beyond the latter, the serrated line of shadows were advancing, the summits still glowing bright in the level rays of sunshine. Beyond the Inyo Mountains, extended numerous other ranges, clad in haze suf-fered with sunlight.

But presently, the sun sank in a glowing sky behind the shad-owy peaks of the Great Western Divide. The last rays lingered for a few moments on the topmost peaks and then faded away. A violet band stole up from the eastern horizon and disappeared. Mountain and valley became a somber gray, but soon a great vault of heavens was strewn with glittering stars, and above the castellated Kaweahs in the west hovered views above, bright in the last glow of sunset.

Mt. Muir from Trail Camp (Photo by Andy Zdon)

Descending from my narrow and lofty perch, I walked back along the twisting trail and down the "switch-backs" to my camp.

The glowing stars, the cold grey granite,
the first rosy glow of dawn
over the desert mountains across
the deep Owens Valley.
Rosy glow in the west as the night vanished;
morning shadows on the mountains
to the east.

Journal entry
An ascent of Mt. Whitney by night

UP THE EAST FACE OF WHITNEY

Among mountaineers, second in fascination to the making of first ascents is the finding of new routes up mountains already climbed, especially if these are difficult. As opportunities of accomplishing the former gradually diminish, climbers turn their attention to the discovery of new and more arduous ways of obtaining summits of mountains. Walking or riding being a rather tame mode of reaching them, in their estimations, they are forever seeking new problems of ascent which may match their skill and strength, puny as these may be, compared with the forces of lofty mountains.

Scaleable with comparative ease from the south, west and north, Mt. Whitney, the highest peak in the United States, has lured mountaineers in the quest of a "real climb." Last season a fairly difficult one was found going from the east up a broad chute culminating in a notch on an arete running northward from the peak and giving access to the north face which was followed to the summit. Unsatisfied with the discovery, however they began to consider whether the apparent sheer east face of Mt. Whitney might not be scaled.

It was with this object in view that a party of five motored westward from Lone Pine toward the base of the Sierra Nevada during the forenoon of August 15 of 1931. The group was one of proven climbing ability. It consisted of Dr. Underhill of Harvard University, one of the most expert rockclimbers in the United States; Francis Farquhar of San Francisco, prominent in the activities of the Sierra Club; Jules Eichorn from the same city and Glen Dawson from Los Angeles, both youths, but very skillful in rockclimbing; and the writer of this sketch. It is pertinent too, that the first descent of the new route was made by three Los Angeles youths: Walter Brem, Richard Jones and Glen Dawson, on September 6, 1939.

Having arrived at the end of the road, some eight miles west of Lone Pine, we transferred our baggage from automobiles to the backs of several mules. After a short trudge up the sun-steeped eastern slope of the range, we swung around a shoulder and entered the refreshing coolness and shade of Lone Pine Canyon with the summit of Mt. Whitney looking from its head a few miles directly to the west. Charmed by the alluring seclusion of the gorge with floor shaded by pine and fir; with brook resounding through a canopy of birch and willow, with walls of mellow-hued and pleasingly sculpted granite, we leisurely followed the trail to Hunter's Flat, a distance of about four miles, and continued up switchbacks to the south of it to an elevation of some 9,000 feet above sea level. There the packs were removed from the mules.

After eating luncheon, we fitted our packs on our backs and, abandoning the trail began to pick our way up the North Fork of Lone Pine Creek. Within a few hundred feet we came upon a projecting buttress around which we swung, and began to scramble over broken rocks in the direction of a crevice leading up a steeply-shelving granite slope to a ledge running along the south wall of the gorge. Occasionally we stopped to regale ourselves in the luscious wild currants which grew abundantly among the chaotic talus through which we were passing. Below us the stream bounded along sonorously, hidden from view by a dense growth of birch and maple.

Upon arriving at the foot of the crevice, we scrambled up it as best we could, laden with heavy and bulky packs, to a ledge

Mt. Whitney
(Photo by United States Department of the Navy)

which we followed around a projection. Although the ledge shelved down to a cliff, we strode rapidly along it in our rubber soled shoes, pausing now and then to look down to the floor of the canyon several hundred feet below us, or turning about to gaze eastward through its U-shaped opening and across the wide basin of Owens Valley to the Inyo Mountains — richly colored, glowing in the afternoon sunshine, and with a mass of snowy-white cumulus clouds hovering above them. A scattering of limber pines grew along the lower portion of the shelf and as it gradually ascended, considerable numbers of the foxtail variety began to appear. To our left, a vertical wall of granite rose in places to a height of several hundred feet.

Having reached the upper end of the shelf, we crossed a strip of talus to the border of a glacially-formed basin in which grew a beautiful grove of foxtail pines. Through these we filed along to the margin of a meadow at an altitude of some 10,000 feet. It was a fascinating spot, by craggy peaks and to the west of the great pinnacles and steep walls of Mt. Whitney. Being without a trail and difficult of access, seldom has human foot trodden its secluded recess, although but a few miles from Owens Valley. Presently, the sun sank behind the serrated peaks of Mt. Whitney, suffusing a few clouds that wreathed about their summits, with vivid-hued light.

The ensuing dawn was literally "rosy-fingered," the peaks of Mt. Whitney and those on either side of the cirques glowing in roseate light of marvelous beauty. After a hasty breakfast, we were soon on our way northward across the meadow hoary with frost, to the base of a slope which we ascended to a cleft in the rock up which we scrambled to an apron-like slope of glaciated granite. Across this we picked our way along a series of cracks to a grove of foxtail pine in another basin.

With this behind us, we clambered up the point of a long promontory extending eastward from a shallow basin directly to the east of Mt. Whitney. Along its narrow crest, we sped nimbly to the margin of the upper basin when we halted for a few minutes in order to survey the face of Mt. Whitney, but being able to make little of it, we walked northwestward a few hundred feet to a small lake which afforded a more satisfactory view. After careful scrutiny, a possible route was discovered. At best, however, it would be obviously a difficult one and any one of a number of apparent "gaps" in it might render it impracticable.

Up a steep acclivity sufficiently broken to permit easy progress we steadily climbed to the notch and there were roped up. Dr. Underhill and Glen Dawson were on one rope; Jules Eichorn and myself on the other. The first rope preceded along the shelf, but as feared, it suddenly terminated in a sheer wall. Upon hearing this, the second rope began to scale the face of the gendarme, but this proving rather hazardous, we swung to the right and succeeded in finding a narrow shelf, or rather the edge of an upright rock slab with a crevice behind it, along which we made our way to a notch behind the pinnacle. From this, we descended a few feet, rounded a protruding buttress on narrow ledges, and began to ascend a chute, rather steep but with surface sufficiently roughened to afford good footing.

After an ascent of a few hundred feet we entered an alcove-like recess where further direct advance was barred by a perpendicular wall. There we awaited rope number one which presently arrived and after a short pause climbed over a low ridge into another chimney, rope number two following. Both ropes then clambered up an overhang to a platform. From this, however, progress upward could be made only by climbing a steep and rather precarious crack. Rather than run the risk of a fall we decided to attempt a traverse around a buttress to the left to a slabby chimney beyond it.

As I swung out over the wall below the platform, an apparently firm rock gave way beneath my foot and went crashing down the sheer cliffs directly below, but as no one was in its path and my handholds were good, no harm resulted.

Rope number one then went around the buttress to reconnoiter and after a pause of some time, the other followed. The traverse proved to be one requiring considerable steadiness, as these

Aerial view of the summit shelter on Mt. Whitney
(Photo by Sam Wyatt, China Lake NAWS)

ledges were narrow and there was a thousand feet of nothing below them. As we came around the projection we were confronted by a gap in a ledge with a narrow platform about eight feet below. There was the alternative of stepping across it — as far as a man of medium height could possibly reach, availing himself of rather poor handholds — or dropping down to the platform and climbing the other side of the gap. Some of the members of the party chose one method; some the other.

Once over the break in the ledge, we were obliged to pull ourselves over a rounded rock by clinging to a diagonal crack with our hands while our feet momentarily swung out over the thousand-foot precipice. We attacked a precipitous, slabby wall availing ourselves of narrow ledges for hand and footholds. A few rods of this, however, brought us to a rounded shoulder with a broad couloir above it.

After halting a short time for luncheon, we proceeded up the chimney, zigzagging back and forth as we clambered over and around great granite steps until we were confronted at the upper end of the chimney by a vertical wall about thirty feet in height. At one side of it, however, there was a narrow crevice up which one might scramble. After removing our rucksacks, we squirmed and corkscrewed up it, the last man tying the knapsacks to the rope carried by the first.

Above the couloir, somewhat to our surprise, we encountered rather easy climbing. We therefore unroped and began to ascend to the right toward the summit of Mt. Whitney. Within a few minutes we came within sight of a cairn a little more than two hundred feet above us.

Quickening the speed, we clambered hastily upward, arriving at the summit, considerably elated by the successful accomplishment of the first ascent of Mt. Whitney up its apparently unscaleable eastern face. Francis Farquhar, having ascended the mountain by another route, was there to meet us.

After spending an hour or more on the top of Mt. Whitney, the party separated, three following the trail southward in order to ascend Mt. Muir, while Dr. Underhill and myself proceeded to descend the north face to a notch a few hundred feet below the summit. It was an easy descent along a rocky rib and down a wide chute to the right of it.

After an evening spent consuming enormous quantities of food and lounging about a campfire, we retired to our sleeping bags under nearby foxtail pines solemnly silent beneath a sky spangled with innumerable stars over-arching the mountains that loomed darkly around the basin. On the following morning we made up our packs and proceeded down the canyon, pleased at having added another outstanding climb to the already discovered number in the Sierra Nevada.

THE FIRST ASCENT OF MT. RUSSELL

For several days in the latter part of June, 1926, I was encamped in a grove of foxtail pines on a branch of Wallace Creek, formerly known as East Fork of Kern River. The location was a delightful one, commanding a fine outlook across the broad basin of the Kern to the lofty and picturesque Kaweahs, to the rugged array of peaks that form the Great Western Divide, and to a portion of the Kings-Kern Divide. The days were remarkably beautiful. The sky was usually clear in the morning, but each afternoon great masses of soft, fluffy cumulus clouds would gather about the western peaks. Presently they would float lazily across the blue sky to the peaks along the main crest of the Sierra, where they appeared to linger for a while before drifting eastward to vanish in the dry atmosphere above Owens Valley.

On the morning of the 24th of June, I set out to climb Mount Russell (14,190′). Turning eastward, I gradually ascended the stream and passed through the upper glaciated basins until I reached Tulainyo Lake, at an elevation of 12,865 feet above sea level. This is unique in its location upon the very crest of the range, with no apparent outlet. It is almost circular in form, about half a mile in diameter, and possesses an air of remoteness and isolation not often encountered. Seldom has human foot trodden its almost vegetationless slopes from which rise abruptly several granite peaks, the highest of which is Mount Russell. I had given some consideration to the best method of approaching this mountain. During the previous autumn, from a nearby peak I had noted a narrow ridge, or knife-edge, leading upward toward the summit. Although if was too deeply gashed to permit one to follow its crest, there appeared to be a shelf on the northern side that might perhaps be used to a point not far below the summit. It was with this purpose of reaching this knife-edge that I was making a half-circuit to the east of the peak.

After luncheon, I continued southward over patches of deep snow and across a stretch of rough talus to the base of a ridge which, being only about five hundred feet in height, was soon surmounted. The route ahead looked formidable — at times impossible. To the south the wall dropped abruptly; to the north after descending at a steep angle for a few feet, it fell away sheer. Difficult as it seemed from a distance, nevertheless the way opened up as I progressed. There was always a safe passage and there were always enough protuberances and crevices to afford secure handholds and footholds. Now and then I came to a gash in the ridge through which I looked with a thrill down vertical cliffs, hundreds of feet in height, to the basin below.

After reaching the end of the ledge, a short scramble brought me to the eastern summit of the mountain. Thence a knife-edge extends a few hundred yards to the western peak, which is apparently the higher. The whole summit, in fact, is nothing more than a knife-edge with a high point at either end. Picking my way along the crest or along shelves a short distance below it, I advanced toward the western eminence, which I reached by hoisting myself over some large granite blocks. There was no cairn or other evidence of a previous ascent.

It was just such an eyrie as delights the heart of a mountaineer. Only a few feet in diameter, the summit drops away vertically to the south and the west and at a very steep angle to the north. The view was superb. To the south across a narrow cirque rose the precipitous eastern front and northern flank of Mount Whitney, seen from this point in its imposing aspect. Beyond, to the southeast, was an array of craggy mountains, and westward across the wide basin of the Kern were the stately and imposing Kaweahs and the ragged line of peaks of the Great Western Divide. To the north the eye followed the crest of the Sierra as far as the Palisades, with Goddard, Darwin and Humphreys looming hazy in the distance.

As I sat on the rocky summit in the warm sunshine, the radiant white clouds that lazily passed overhead gradually became denser and assumed a darker hue. Clouds were gathering in threatening masses around the Kaweahs and the Great Western Divide and seemed to be moving in mass upon a peak west of Mount Russell. Mindful of previous unpleasant encounters with electric storms on mountain-tops, I considered it time to seek lower elevations. Returning to the eastern summit I paused, debating whether I should follow the route used in the ascent or attempt a descent down an arete to the north. I decided upon the latter course, although it might entail a return to the summit. There was still a good deal of snow on the north face. To avoid the glaciated slopes that cover a good portion of that side of the mountain, I followed the crest of the knife-edge or made my way along shelves immediately to the west of it. In the meantime, the storm passed harmlessly by.

On the whole, less difficulty was encountered in the descent than I had anticipated. The joint-planes of the rock were rather far apart, and it was sometimes necessary to make a rather long drop in getting down from some huge block. Eventually a rather formidable wall appeared to bar farther progress. On one side was a vertical cliff, on the other a steeply shelving slope; but by an assortment of gymnastic maneuvers familiar to every rock-climber I was able to let myself down in safety to the base of this obstacle. Thence I sped down a snow-slope, hurried onward along a stream, past a lake, and safely reached my camp in the grove of foxtail pines near the base of Mount Barnard.

Temple Crag (Photo by Vern Clevenger)

TEMPLE CRAG IN NOVEMBER

Temple Crag

One of the most beautiful and striking of all the craggy peaks of the Sierra Nevada is Temple Crag (Mt. Alice), an outlying spur of the Palisade Group, 13,016 feet in elevation. From the north across the canyon of Big Pine Creek, its deeply-fluted face and sharp pinnacles instantly attract the eye by their finely and sublimely sculptured forms. Although greatly surpassed in height by the nearby Palisades, it is unexcelled by any of them in boldness and beauty of outline. Its summit, scaled but few times, commands a magnificent view of the long line of serrated Palisades that sweep in a crescent to the south and west, forming an assemblage of lofty peaks whose rugged alpine grandeur is not surpassed by any group of mountains in the Sierra.

To those for whom the mountains are something more than objects to be looked at, inspiring as that may be, they are always a challenge, especially when their summits promise a wide outlook and their ascent is somewhat difficult. Temple Crag belongs to this class. From it, one obtains a sublime view and scaling it is somewhat of a feat in rock-climbing. Its north face is obviously unscaleable and it has been ascended but few times from its southern and eastern sides.

On an evening in early November, I came up to a shelter cabin near its base, intending to visit the Palisade Glacier on the following day. However, when ready to start on this errand on the following morning, my eye was attracted by the precipices and pinnacles of Temple Crag and the lure exacted by them was too strong to resist, so that I immediately began to climb toward a notch between it and an unnamed mountain to the east of it. The steep slope leading up to it was buried in the broken rocks which increased in size as I advanced. About a foot of soft snow also impeded my progress, but I could often avoid this by springing from one rock to another. Reaching the saddle, across a deep canyon and above a glacier, loomed Middle Palisade, 14,051 feet in elevation, and to the southeast were the other massive and broken peaks not greatly inferior to it in height.

Pausing for a few minutes, I deliberated as to what would be my next step. As I disliked to drop down into the basin below and attack the crag from the north, I carefully scanned the steep rock face just above me. At first it appeared so sheer as to afford no opportunity for an ascent, but upon further scrutiny, I noted a cleft about fifty feet in height, which if negotiable would lead up to what appeared to be a diagonal shelf and that to the crest of a ridge that might lead to the summit. Approaching its base, I noted sufficient hand and footholds to render an ascent possible, and after attaching my knapsack and ice ax to a rope, I proceeded to scale it. As there proved to be nothing that would stop a good rock climber, I steadily hoisted myself from hold to hold, and at convenient intervals drew up my impediments after me. As anticipated, it opened out on a broken shelf that ascended rapidly to a ridge a short distance above, while from the latter a slope of broken rock slope extended upward almost to the summit, perhaps a thousand feet higher. Fortunately, this portion of the mountain was free from snow. There was no wind and the sun above shone warm on the rocky face of the mountain. As I rose steadily along the main crest, the view became more and more striking. To my right the mountain broke away in sheer precipices many hundreds of feet in height. Just below the summit, the crest narrowed to a knife-edge a few feet in width with

Gnarled pine (Photo by Andy Zdon)

vertical drops and walls hundreds of feet in depth on either side. Although a shelf was in one place only a few inches in width, both the footholds and the handholds were so safe that one could look down into the gulf below with perfect equanimity. The summit, only a few feet in diameter, broke away in a great notch beyond which was another jagged peak. To the south and west, the view was cut off by the long, serrated line of the Palisades, three of which rise to an altitude of over 14,000 feet above sea-level. Below these dark, craggy forms was a series of glaciers which added greatly to the alpine setting of the panorama, whose rugged, craggy sublimity has few equals in the United States. Fascinated by it, the eye repeatedly follows the array of magnificence from one end to the other. Beginning from the northwest, the most prominent peaks are Agassiz Needle, Mt. Winchell, the North Palisade, Mt. Sill and the Middle Palisade. The most inspiring of these are the North and the Middle Palisades followed by Mt. Sill. With the exception of the Middle Palisade, all can be scaled from the glaciers at their base. Agassiz Needle, up its northeasterly and southeasterly faces; Mt. Winchell up its eastern side; the North Palisade up a snow chute, over a cliff and along the arete to the summit. None of these is a particularly easy climb and two of them — that of the northeast face of Agassiz Needle and that of the North Palisade — are unusually difficult. To the north and northwest the upper basin of Big Pine Creek with its undulating, sparsely wooded area, dotted with a dozen or more alpine lakes, formed an agreeable contrast to their rugged environs. Northeast of the basin was a rounded ridge and beyond that a rolling plateau, a remnant of an ancient landscape, untouched by glacial action. To the east and northeast are the White Mountains, a lofty mass culminating in a peak of the same name attaining an elevation of 14,242 feet above sea-level.

The sunshine fell warm on the crag and there was silence except for the faint, far away sound of falling water, the distant call of the Clark crow and occasionally, the murmur of the wind about the hollow flanks of the peak. After contemplating for some time, the sublime and beautiful panorama that encircled my isolated vantage point, I began the descent. Hurrying down the steep slope below the final pinnacle while springing from rock to rock, I had a nasty fall from one overturning with me, luckily suffering no injury except a battered chin. The return, below the notch was a combination of rock-leaping and wading or sometimes floundering through the snow.

Arriving at the cabin, I quickly threw together articles which I had left there and was soon on my way down the trail. Afternoon shadows already extended far down over the mountains. My way led through stretches of tamarack pine, across meadows, now brown and sere, along streams which hurried along beneath leafless birch and willow. As the elevation decreased, a scattering growth of large yellow pines grew on the valley floor and the rocky slopes rising from it. When nearing the end of the trail, I looked up a broad and beautiful canyon to the southwest at the head of which, above its glacier-clad base, the Middle Palisade loomed high in the gathering twilight.

Figure on top of Muir hut.
(Photo by Cedric Wright, The Bancroft Library)

OVER THE HERMIT

Some thirty of us filed out of camp over the swollen water of Evolution Creek on a pine tree felled across it, and began to diagonal upward across a slope rich with an open stand of lodgepole and white-bark pines. After climbing a moderately steep rise of a few hundred feet, we entered a canyon which sloped gently upward for several miles toward high peaks some distance to the south.

A short distance to the southeast, a beautiful peak with the form of a tapering sugar loaf rose to an altitude of over 12,000 feet. Although not nearly so high as some of the nearby peaks, it affords an excellent climb and a superb view from its narrow summit.

After climbing for perhaps a mile across alleviating strips of lodgepole pines and meadows, we began to climb obliquely upward over the lower slopes of the west face of the Hermit. Gradually the timber grew smaller and more scattered until, as we began to pick our way along and up over ledges on a precipitous shoulder of the mountain, nothing now remained but dwarfed and contorted white-bark pines, only a few feet in height.

After surveying around the shoulder and above the head of a large steep chute, we veered to the left and began to climb one of a number of narrow granite ribs on that face of the mountain. They afforded interesting climbing and there was less danger from falling rocks than in the chutes below them.

Within an hour or so, we came out in a deep gash in the narrowed and sharply dentate arete or ridge running southward from the top of the mountain which was then no great distance from us to the north. Pushing upward, we edged along minor ledges and clambered upward over great steep and sometimes vertical pitches.

Within a short time, we came to the foot of the final rock, a granite monolith perhaps twenty feet in height. From the north, one could climb to within a few feet of the top of this, but the last pitch being too long for one's reach, it was necessary to employ the "courte echelle" or two-man stand in which one person clambered onto the shoulder of another and with this assistance was able to hoist himself to the top of the rock, an area of a few square yards.

According to mountaineering ethics, with the exception of a few dangerous conditions, one cannot claim the ascent of a mountain unless he stands, sits on or at least lies across the actual summit. To reach it with one's hands is not sufficient. Almost all of the party were eager to stand on the actual summit and to sign their names in the register on it.

Clambering over the shoulders of one of the stronger members of the party and secured from above by a rope, one after another, men and women in about equal number, made the short but precipitous escalade to the top and after a stay of a few minutes, returned. Only a portion of them had reached the top, when threatening clouds began to appear above, and got dark only a few miles to the south. They might reach the top of the Hermit within a very short time, yet a storm on the top of such a mountain peak as that on which we were standing was not a thing to be trifled with.

All but the last few had gotten up and returned, however, when a heavy wind began to sweep across the narrow summit, and we were enveloped in a snow squall. Fearing that an electric storm might develop within a few minutes, I appointed two deputy leaders and started them down the side of the mountain opposite that of which we had come.

Within ten minutes, the last of the party, had gotten up and down the monolith. I followed the two advance groups for some distance down the mountain to a point where they had veered, one to the left, the other to the right. The latter, had gone down a chute and apparently was in difficulty. Fearing that it might have come to a high vertical drop-off as sometimes happens in such chutes, I appointed another deputy leader and indicated a route by which he should be able to get off the mountain without difficulty. I followed the other down the deep chute.

Although not actually "hung up," they were having a rather difficult time of it, partly from an abundance of loose rock, partly from occasional drop-offs which, though not unscaleable, they were to say the least not easy, especially for those with little experience in climbing as was the case with some members of the party.

By careful maneuvering, however, to avoid rocks being dislodged by those above on those below, and by the use of the rope on one or two of the drop-offs, the party eventually reached the mouth of the chute. Meanwhile, the first of the advance parties had swung around the shoulder of the mountain to the left, and the "rear guard" which I had been bringing down, had not yet appeared, so I directed the one which had emerged from the chute, down to a basin some three hundred feet below, while I swung around the base of the steep slopes to a good vantage point where I stopped and waited.

Within a short while I observed them making their way slowly, but steadily down the steep front of the mountain. As they were obviously not in any difficulty, I simply watched them until they came out the mouth of a chute, a short distance to one side.

I then hastened down to the basin to which I had directed the second party, which meanwhile had gone on. All the rear guard having assembled in the basin after stopping along a stream and eating a second or third luncheon, we began to file down the stream.

Although we were off the upper portion of the peak, we were by no means off the mountain. Below us lay a tier of cliffs, perhaps a thousand feet in height. To get down over this without becoming hung up and forced to make a detour — perhaps a long one — would require careful maneuvering. After some experience with rock, one seems, however, to acquire a sort of instinct which is I suppose a sort of subconscious after effect of numerous similar experiences, so that he is usually able to thread his way down without encountering insurmountable obstacles.

For some distance we headed directly downward and then instinctively sensing sheer cliffs ahead, I went out on a vantage point and looked around. The cliffs directly below probably were impassable, but no great distance to the right, a steep slope led down though cliffs on either side.

We moved toward this horizontally, and within only a few minutes we were again on our way directly downward. Scattered trees began to appear and in places, on the top slopes was an abundance of flowers, cassiope or white heather, were in full bloom, displaying thousands of waxen white pendants, Lilly of the Valley-like blossoms. In years of rambling through the Sierra, I had never seen a finer display of this, perhaps the most beautiful flower of the high Sierra.

Within no great while, we reached the floor of the canyon below us, and with the exception of an occasional strip of talus fallen from the cliffs above, our way now lay through grassy meadows for about a mile and thence through a strip of pines and over a small undulating area of glaciated granite to camp. After recrossing Evolution Creek on the same pine, we strode into camp, and there found that the other two parties had also ably reached it. Thirty people over the top of The Hermit and back into camp without mishap, despite rather numerous obstacles encountered, was a feat of which the party might well congratulate themselves.

A STORMY ASCENT OF MT. HUMPHREYS

My camp was on the lee of a small, densely branched white-bark pine about four hundred yards west of Piute Pass, at an elevation of over 11,000 feet on the main crest of the Sierra. Nearby, a small stream bounded melodiously by, coming from snowfields only a short distance above. Its borders were given with fresh grass and lush wild cyclamen that were hooking up rapidly to take advantage as quickly as possible of the short summers that they obtain at these lofty elevations. It was then toward the end of June.

From a point only a few rods distant to the east, to the southward I looked down on a typical high Sierra basin contouring two beautiful lakes gleaming a bright sapphire in a setting of glaciated undulating terrain sprinkled with a scattering of white bark pine. Across it there was a handsome pyramided mountain, as yet unnamed, while to the northeast stood the couloir-fluted south face of Mt. Emerson, its summit extending eastward along a line of red spires.

A violent wind had swept across the crest of the Sierra on the preceding day — so violent that it had forced me to desist from the ascent of a nearby peak. But the morning being calm, I went out at an early hour toward Mt. Humphreys, towering in a great rugged pyramid, from the crest of the Sierra, several miles distant. Snow still covered most of the undulating landscape. Along a rounded ridge which I followed for a considerable distance, there were some spaces free from snow, in which, Draba, a diminutive member of the mustard family, was already displaying clusters of vivid yellow flowers.

The sky was cloudless and a stainless blue, and for awhile the atmosphere was perfectly calm. I passed several lakes upon

The northeast face of Mt. Humphreys
(Photo by Norman Clyde, Eastern California Museum Collection)

which the ice had begun to break, but as I approached Mt. Humphreys the depth of the snow gradually increased, and as I reached the latter I heard a muffled roar which I thought might come from a stream flowing underneath the snow, in one or other of the steep chutes that ran up the precipitous south face of the mountain. A heavy wind beat against the north face of the mountain and swept past the summit pyramid that towered some five hundred-feet above the part upon which I was standing.

Beyond a notch, a deep chute ran about halfway up the west face. This was followed in the ascent of the couloir to a well-broken face, several hundred feet in height to the right. This was followed by an escalade up a steep and almost vertical wall perhaps seventy-five feet in height. From the top of the wall, a narrow rockclimb runs upward to the summit of Mt. Humphreys, perhaps fifty yards distant.

In reaching the final pyramid, one would be sheltered from the wind in the deep couloir and above it he could be almost entirely on the lee-side of the mountain. Upon reaching the top of the wall, however, he would be exposed to the full violence of the wind and to attempt to continue up the cockscomb only several feet wide in places and falling away sheer on either side for hundreds of feet would be nothing short of foolhardy.

As anticipated, I reached the top of the wall without encountering any special difficulty. There I was exposed to the full force of the wind which swept past with almost the velocity of a gale. Sweeping to the right, on the side of the mountain, I sought shelter from the wind, and found it on a narrow ledge, at least partially protected from the fierce blast.

Although this tempest was none to warm, from this aerial peak I enjoyed a superb view for the sky was cloudless and the atmosphere clear southward along the crest of the highest peaks of the Sierra terminating in the loftiest summit, that of Mt. Whitney some fifty miles distant. This was indeed doubly impressive by the large quantity of snow in the mountains, particularly on the northern faces and slopes.

For several hours, I waited hoping that the wind might drop sufficiently to enable me to continue to the top of the mountain without running too great a risk of being blown from it by the gale-like wind. The latter, however, seemed to increase rather than decrease in violence. I therefore retraced my way down from the face of the mountain and back across the undulating terrain of Mt. Humphreys basin to my camp.

On the following morning, the weather was again beautifully calm. Unwilling to be thwarted in my proposed ascent of Mt. Humphreys, I again set out for the mountain. The wind again arose and masses of vapor, presaging a storm began to gather about its summits. Not wishing to be thwarted again, I quickened my pace and ascended to the crest of the west ridge, and to the base of the first pyramid in rapid time.

By the time clouds were banked up to the north of the mountain and streamed eastward from the summit, white snowflakes were borne past me by a wind which fortunately was not nearly so strong as that of the preceding day.

I therefore hurried up the deep chute, clambered up the steep broken face to the right of it, scaled the precipitous wall and struck out eastward along the crest of the cockscomb leading to the summit of the mountain, then little more than a stone's throw.

Meanwhile the clouds thickened, at times cutting off from view the range below, over which they were gradually settling. Snow squalls flurried past covering the rock with a light coating of snow.

Advancing rapidly, within a few minutes I reached the highest point of the mountain, where I paused for a few moments to survey the cloud-enveloped Sierra, stretching far to the south and the north. The wind, however, was likely to increase and the falling snow to render the rock slippery. I hastily removed the register from the cairn on the top of the mountain, signed it, replaced it in the cairn and turning about began to retrace my way down the precipitous mountain.

Reaching the latter without mishap, I struck out southward across the undulating terrain. I had not gone far however, before masses of clouds had almost completely enveloped Mt. Humphreys, and by the time that I reached camp they were rapidly closing down upon it. Presently, snow began to fall in great flakes so briskly that one could only see a few rods.

Hurriedly packing sleeping bag and accessories, I was soon trudging upward toward Piute Pass. The latter reached, I hastened down the eastern escarpment of the Sierra. Soon, however, the volume of clouds began to shift and break away, affording glorious glimpses of rugged mountains peering though cloud masses rendered luminous by the afternoon sun that shone brightly upon them. But the snow continued to fall as I hastened down the canyon, even down to the grove of aspen some 1,500 feet below the pass, then in the full beauty of new foliage.

Clyde Minaret (Photo by Pete Yamagata)

HIGHEST OF THE MINARETS

From my camp at Thousand Island Lake, one morning in the latter part of June, I set forth on a ramble southward. Crossing a ridge a few hundred feet in height, I dropped down to Garnet Lake, an extremely beautiful one, oval in form, a mile or more in length, shut in to the north and south by rocky ridges; and to the west by the magnificently picturesque form of Mt. Banner rising in sheer walls to an elevation slightly under 13,000 feet above sea-level. A brisk wind ruffled its azure water causing it to break energetically against its rocky shores, which rises abruptly in massive granite varied by scattered stands of lodgepole pine and mountain hemlock.

Having surmounted a second ridge, I began to descend into the valley of Shadow Creek. To the southwest, across the forested canyon, rose the jagged Minarets, seeming to utter a challenge as I gazed at them for they had never been scaled from the eastern side and but once from the western one. Below and some distance to the left lay Shadow Lake, a blue expanse of water in a setting of green conifers and gray granite walls. Upon reaching the floor of the valley, I was surprised by its beauty. A limpid stream of considerable volume plunged in snowy cascades, raced along in scintillating rapids and lingered in deep emerald pools. On either side stood groves of lodgepole pine with mountain hemlock interspersed in increasing numbers as one advanced up the valley. A second lake, deep, clear and blue presently came within view, its beauty enhanced by an alpine setting of the pinnacled Minarets to the southwest and by the dark, massive peaks of Mts. Ritter and Banner to the northwest. Above its sapphire depths stood a grove of very large mountain hemlocks — one of the finest in the Sierra. Entering it, I stopped for a short time on a bed of red heather which seemed to be more abundant there than almost anywhere in the Sierra. I could not refrain from admiring the rugged beauty of the mature hemlocks and the elegant grace of the young ones — most beautiful of all our alpine conifers.

Continuing on my way, I crossed a stream meandering through grassy meadows; climbed a green slope to the crest of a rocky ridge from which I looked down to the left on Iceberg Lake, of deepest blue and sunk in a bowl-like amphitheater with a fine grove of mountain hemlock on one side and a precipitous glacier on the other. From time to time, even in midsummer, large fragments of ice break away, fall into and float around in the ultramarine blue of the lake — hence the name of Iceberg Lake.

The ridge became rockier and snow was soon encountered as I pressed toward the Minarets which seemed to entice me onward. The highest of them was directly to the south and rose apparently sheer from a precipitous hanging glacier. Presently, I came to the latter and began to trudge up a slope that became steeper as I advanced. The sun was already dropping westward and shadows were falling across the glacier from jagged pinnacles to the right. Steeply inclined frozen snow soon obliged me to cut steps around a protruding parapet, for a distance of several hundred feet. This passed, the gradient became gentler and being still exposed to the sunshine was sufficiently soft to enable me to progress rapidly.

Upon reaching the upper side of the glacier immediately below the highest Minaret, I spent a short time exploring the bergschrund and then pausing for a few minutes, considered my further plans. It was already four o'clock. If an attempt were made to climb the peak it might be unsuccessful, but even if it should be, the surface of the glacier would be frozen hard upon my return, obliging me to cut my way down, perhaps in darkness, a tedious and somewhat precarious undertaking.

Deciding to make the attempt, however, I found a bridge across the bergschrund and with some little difficulty, clambered up the rocks directly above it. Thence, I worked my way upward along narrow shelves and over steep pitches, sometimes hoisting myself with little more than a finger and a toehold, wondering whether I should be able to make the descent so readily. Eventually, I reached the crest only to find a deep gash between me and the highest point. As a descent to the former would be somewhat hazardous, I hastened down a ridge paralleling a couloir for about two hundred feet. In my hurry, I almost incurred an accident. As I stepped on an apparently firm slab, it gave way, but fortunately a good handhold prevented me from going along with it. Striking my ice axe and rucksack which had been let down over a vertical pitch, I came within an ace of pushing them over the mountainside — a serious possibility, for without an ice axe I would be unable to cross the glacier by night.

Eventually finding a shelf leading to the bottom of the couloir, I followed it thither. Although very steep, plenty of handholds enabled me to scale it and the wall above it with considerable speed. Presently, I swung up to the crest, only a few yards from the summit. It was indeed an eyrie. Only a few feet in diameter, it dropped away sheer for hundreds of feet on every side except the one up which I had climbed. The sun, nearing the horizon, cast horizontal rays across the Sierra, stretching far southward. From every peak, elongated shadows were creeping eastward. To the north, a line of jagged pinnacles, not much lower than the one on which I was standing, extended toward the rugged form of Mt. Ritter, looming ruggedly against the blue sky. To the left of it stood the picturesque groups of Mts. Lyell, McClure and Rodgers, their summits lighted up by the evening rays of the sun.

Soon I was on my way down the wall, the couloir and along the shelf. By descending somewhat to the east of the route of the ascent some of the difficulties incurred in the former were avoided, in fact, few were encountered until I neared the glacier. There, a good deal of time was spent in finding a way down the steep, smooth rock immediately above the glacier. The latter, as anticipated, was already frozen hard and darkness was fast settling

Clyde Minaret through the rain (Photo by Pete Yamagata)

down on the mountains. About an hour was consumed in cutting my way across the glacier and around the buttress, but as there was a thousand feet of steeply inclined snow and ice below, it was not advisable to hurry. Picking my way slowly and carefully down a broken cliff, I came at length to a clump of white-bark pine with a nearby lake gleaming through the darkness. As there was plenty of fuel, I decided to bivouac for the night, although being on a pass, it would be more or less exposed to the wind. It did blow heavily all night and the temperature was rather frigid, but the dense growth of trees broke the violence of the wind, while a blazing bonfire dispelled the cold. The moon shed a half-radiance of the battlemented Minarets to the west and the dark forms of Ritter and Banner silhouetted against the starry sky to the north — a sight of fascinating alpine sublimity.

At daybreak, I left my bivouac, passed the lake — a beautiful sheet of limpid blue, shining like a mirror in the dawn — descended a pitch a few hundred feet high, passed the exquisite Iceberg Lake, and swung across the meadows to Lake Ediza. There, I ate the remainder of the lunch which I had brought with me from camp on the preceding day and enjoyed a nap on a sunny bed of heather. Although hungry, I decided to return to camp over the top of Mt. Ritter, 13,156 feet above sea-level, by dropping down its northern face and swinging around Mt. Banner and Thousand Island Lake.

After traversing the grove of hemlocks and crossing an alpine meadow down which came numerous brooks fed by the abundant snow and the glacier above, I clambered up the glaciated benches of a cliff several hundred feet in height and trudged across a small glacier to a couloir opening on to it from the north. Up this I turned, making my way at first on snow, then over the rocks. These I found interesting from the great variety of igneous constituents present in them. Very interesting also were the views obtained of the black pinnacles of the Minarets immediately below and of the southern Sierra looming vast in the distance. Eventually, the chute widened, opening up on a gradual slope leading up to the summit which I reached about noon.

The day was an extremely pleasant one and the view, magnificent, extending far down the axis of the range and including most of its major peaks. Near at hand across the deep gorge of the North Fork of the San Joaquin, the Mt. Lyell group stood sharply outlined against a cerulean sky. To the northeast, past the Davis group, gleamed the gray-green expanse of Mono Lake in a setting of tawny desert waste.

After a short pause, I went down the north face of the peak, then down a broad couloir which ended in a steep snow slope to the saddle between Mts. Ritter and Banner. Veering to the right, I sped down the snow around the shoulder of the latter and then picked my way down over the rocks to Thousand Island Lake. While walking across the soft meadow and around the rocky margin of the lakes I was fascinated by the alpine beauty of the scene. Behind rose the steep-walled north face of Mt. Banner, one of the most picturesque mountains in the Sierra, enveloped in afternoon shadows and crowned with massive white clouds. To my right lay the lake, a scintillating sheet of sapphire dotted with rocky islets, a mile or more in diameter.

OVER UNICORN AND CATHEDRAL PEAKS: THE YOSEMITE NATIONAL PARK

Several miles southward from the Tuolumne Meadows, stand a number of sharp granite peaks, unique in the Sierra or anywhere else for that matter, for their striking form. Two of them, Unicorn and Cathedral Peaks are viable from the Meadows. The former owes its name to the fact that from a number of angles, its long summit crest is terminated to the west by a sharp pinnacle having some slight resemblance to a horn. Cathedral Peak, also a very beautiful mountain, likewise owes its name to the fact that from numerous angles — it is strikingly like a great cathedral surmounted by a slender spire.

These sharp peaks are not only picturesque to view but also afford excellent, and for the most part, not inordinately difficult or dangerous ascents to those fond of rock climbing. The most accessible and the most popular of these spires are Unicorn and Cathedral Peaks. Either can be reached, ascended and a return made to the Meadows within a few hours, or both can be ascended in a single and not a very long day.

One of a number of my visits to these peaks was made in the early part of August, accompanied by an engineer, Mr. B.H. Moulder, from Los Angeles. Leaving the tourist camp about a mile south of Lembert Dome, we followed a trail leading southwestward to Elizabeth Lake at the north base of Unicorn Peak. As the trail gradually climbs from the meadows, it passes through an open stand of tamarack pine, many of which for a space of a mile or so have unfortunately been killed by an insect pest. With a feeling of relief one enters the forest untouched by the latter. One is pleased also by the appearance of a scattering of alpine hemlocks, perhaps the most beautiful of our mountain conifers, especially the exceedingly graceful young trees with their drooping boughs and pendant tops. Their needles are of a most agreeable blue-green hue and at this time, great numbers of small purplish cones hung from the arching boughs.

For a few minutes, we passed in the grassy margin of Elizabeth Lake perhaps a quarter of a mile in diameter and like most Sierra Lakes, a limpid blue. Around the northwestward shore of the lake we then continued to the foot of Unicorn Peak. The gradient steepened and presently grass and heather-clad slopes were succeeded by rather precipitous inclines of granite. As we were wearing basketball shoes, we very easily picked our way along ledges and up sheltering slopes of clean, dry granite. Much of this was smooth, fine grained rock, a light-colored rock going by the name of Johnson granite. Farther up we traversed a strip of a coarser granite variety with numerous large crystals of feldspar in it, and from the fact that a large portion of Cathedral Peak is composed of it, it is termed Cathedral granite.

On the lower and middle portion of the slope we passed several extremely beautiful groves of hemlock. These however, soon dwindled in size together with a number of white-bark pine, the most typical timberline tree of the Sierra. The firm rock which afforded some pleasant climbing, as we approached the saddle to the left of the pinnacle forming the highest portion of the mountain, was succeeded by disintegrated granite.

Soon we reached the crest, a narrow rib of granite broken into masonry-like blocks. Along them we picked our way, now and then working around clumps of dense, white-bark pine stunted and dwarfed by the inclement conditions to which it was exposed during many years. In a few minutes, we were at the notch immediately below the summit pinnacle. The climbing became interesting as we walked along narrow ledges dropping away and sheer to the left for several hundred feet and hoisted ourselves up vertical pitches. In one place, a gap occurred in a ledge and an overhang leaned out over this in a somewhat embarrassing fashion. It was necessary to reach around the latter and grasp crevices in the rocks beyond and then swing around.

Unicorn (left) and the pointed summit of Cathedral Peak (distant right) from Soda Springs with old cabin, in Tuolumne Meadows. (Photo by Andy Zdon)

Above this, several steep pitches brought us to the crest, a knife-edge several feet in diameter which we followed to the summit, a matter of only a few rods. Although only 10,849 feet in altitude, it commands a great portion of the Yosemite Park. To the northwest, only a few miles distant were the red-hued and rounded forms of Mt. Dana and Gibbs; to the southeast, Mt. Lyell and other almost equally rugged and striking peaks around it; to the north across Tuolumne Meadows was the rough-hewn Mt. Conness with its pleasing light-colored granite, while to the left of it was the extreme, broken area between the Grand Canyon of the Tuolumne and the crest forming the north boundary of the Park.

For upwards of an hour, we ate luncheon and loitered about on the narrow summit. As it was still early in the afternoon, we then decided to climb Cathedral Peak, little more than a mile distant to the west in an air line. For the sake of variety, however, we went down the north face of the pinnacle. As most of this steep, slabby rock afforded few holds, it was both easier and safer to "rope down" most of the way, only about a hundred feet in all. After adjusting a loop of light rope around a rock and then threading our alpine rope through it, we then adjusted the doubled rope around our bodies so as to form a sliding brake and then walked backwards down an incline of perhaps forty degrees. Several repetitions of this brought us to the base of the pinnacle.

We then advanced to the saddle, crossed it and descended the southwest face of the peak to the basin below it. As we gradually swung to the right toward Cathedral Peak, we encountered bluffs several hundred feet in height, which required some maneuvering as we pushed our way along the none too frequent ledges along its face. The last one was sloping and grassy-covered and as we had brought neither nailed shoes nor ice axe we tread very gingerly along it, as it led diagonally down to the base of the cliff.

Below the latter, we moved around the margin of a deep, blue lake lying on the floor of a basin and then up though an open growth of tamarack pine to the east base of the northeast slope of Cathedral Peak. For perhaps a thousand feet, we switchbacked up a gradually steepening incline sometimes on lone "granite sand" but more often on hard clean granite sloping at a considerable angle.

Eventually, we reached the crest, a narrow knife-edge which was followed southward several hundred feet to the base of the pinnacle forming the summit of the peak. Across the steeply pitching west face of this, availing ourselves of shelves in many cases only a few inches wide, for several hundred feet. We then went almost directly upward for a short distance and then followed ledges to the northwestern face of the first pinnacle where another ledge carried us to the right of a gap immediately on the other side of it. Through the gap we scrambled to a sort of alcove with a deeply corrugated floor sloping down to the bank of a cliff to the right. From this, the ascent to the top is usually made up the face of the rock by availing oneself of two deep parallel cracks some two feet apart. By inserting hands and feet in each of these, the climber hoists himself up to the top of the spire, somewhat airy but a few feet in diameter.

After a brief sojourn on this, we descended several long steps as it were, to the left of the cracks, to a short chimney, down which we went over an overhang to the alcove, then across this and through the gap.

In the descent, we went obliquely down the west face of the peak, sometimes pushing our way along steeply inclined bare naked granite; at other times through low matted growths of white bark pine. Eventually, we swung somewhat to the right so as to intersect a ridge running northwestward from the mountain, by following the crest of which the foot of the peak was quickly gained.

We then struck out northeastward through the forest. By this time the sunshine of late afternoon was streaming through the conifer boughs of the mountain hemlock, flecking their great red-brown trunks with bright light, seeming all the brighter from the deep shade by which it was surrounded. Around a meadow there was an unusual number of young hemlocks, extremely graceful with their slender, spirey forms and nodding crests. Some of the smaller trees were laden with a wreath of purple cones.

Within a mile, we intersected the Sunrise Trail, in our case more of a "sunset" one, down which we strode to the meadows and along them to camp. This terminating a delightfully interesting, somewhat, but not overly strenuous day in the Yosemite Park.

Ansel Adams gets a tripod belay across a stream on
one of Clyde's Sierra Club High Trips
(Photo by Cedric Wright, The Bancroft Library)

CO-OPERATION IN CAMPING

"Is the axe sharp?" inquired my companion in camping as I busied myself cutting a supply of wood.

"No, not especially so," I replied.

Probably the man in question, not being of the co-operative kind, would not have taken the trouble to wield the axe even if it had been in perfect condition. Anyway, the dullness of the only available one served as a sufficient alibi for letting someone else do all the wood cutting during the entire trip.

This is only one example of the camp ethics of many campers whom I have observed, and perhaps only too frequently have camped with. One is surprised that they do not adopt at least a 50-50 system of co-operation, since only by such can a camping party realize the maximum of pleasure on a trip. Even if the other members of the party may, with at least apparently good grace, do virtually all of the camp work and chores, it is scarcely fair to them, and if they are not gifted with an unusual amount of patience and forbearance, may eventually result in an explosion of some sort, with consequent strained camp relations, or possibly the breaking up of the camp. Either of these alternatives is, of course, to be deplored, and is generally, at least at a later date, regretted by both parties.

There are situations on every camping trip in which, if every member of the party "pitches in," as it were, doing his share, and is not afraid of doing more, the work with which a party is confronted will be accomplished in a remarkably short time. In establishing camp, for example, tents may need to be pitched, wood and water be gotten, and if pack and saddle animals are used, these must be unpacked and taken to pasture. If every member of a party does what he is best fitted to do, all the work may be done with surprising celerity.

As a contrast, I might mention two different parties. One night three of us came to camp late. Despite the fact that wood and water had to be gotten, trout had to be cleaned, a fire built, and a meal cooked, my two companions "flopped down" on the ground.

The other was a case of a couple with whom I traveled for several weeks in the Sierra Nevada. Immediately upon arriving at a camp site in the afternoon or evening, I helped my friend unpack and unsaddle his stock. This done, he led the animals to pasture, while I picked up the axe and set about getting in a supply of wood, his wife meanwhile getting the food out of the kyacks. Enough wood to start the evening meal gotten, I filled the buckets with water, and then set about cutting more wood, either for the cooking or the bonfire. In less than an hour after our reaching camp, all the necessary chores were done and the evening meal cooked and ready to eat. Had we not co-operated, double the time would probably have been necessary to establish camp and prepare dinner. One is always pleased to go on a camping trip with such people as these were, but is likely to be rather indifferent as to whether he makes a second trip with persons who comport themselves as did the two members of the other party.

COMFORTABLE BIVOUACKING

It pays to spend ten or fifteen minutes in making a good bed, said a stockman to me on the occasion of my first visit to the high mountains of the west. I was a bit surprised knowing that stockmen, as a rule, follow a "flop" down anywhere habit.

However, when camping in the open, under me is a pneumatic or other form of mattress, ten minutes in preparing. A comfortable sleeping place may mean a night of sound or unsound sleep. With plenty to eat and plenty of sound sleep it is surprising how much the human physique can endure. Deprived of either and the strongest will soon suffer. He may endure for a surprising length of time, but why undergo suffering which in most camping conditions is unnecessary.

In the absence of a mattress, dry leaves or pine needles of some sort are often available. It is surprising, however, how often the camper will fail to avail himself of these. Once, for example, while out on a weekend trip, one young fellow was camped on the floor of a canyon. Supper over, my friend curled up on a rock and remained there until morning. Perhaps he slept soundly, but the choice of a granite boulder as a mattress was a bit surprising, when dry maple leaves lay to a depth of a foot or more, within ten feet of the rock on which he bivouacked.

Dry leaves of deciduous trees serve such a purpose well. In the conifer belts, boughs of the pine are better. In a few minutes, the camper can often rake up enough to make a "bed" six or eight inches deep. This of course as a rule not in public camp.

If one has sufficient time, and is in a location where green pine, or more preferably fir boughs can be cut, an excellent bed can be found by weaving these under side of the needles up and the better of the boughs toward the head of the bed. In the absence of leaves of any kind, it is important that the material on which one rests be conformed to the contour of the body. In soil, particularly hard soil, some digging tool may be necessary. A mountaineer sometimes uses his ice axe for this purpose. In the absence of a tool, by looking about, one can often find a spot that will "fit" pretty well.

The selection of a location is also of some importance. Cold, damp air tends to settle down or flow along meadows, lakes and streams. A difference of a hundred feet of elevation often will make an appreciable difference in the warmth and dryness of the air. In the case of a heavy wind, behind a log, rock or tree often affords considerable protection. Overhead, a thick broad evergreen will shed an abounding amount of rain or snow. In the Rockies, the blue and Engelmann spruce and the balsam fir are especially efficient in this respect. At timberline, in most of the high ranges of the west, snug sleeping places can with little trouble be made beneath the dense boughs of the dwarfed forms of pines, fir and hemlock found growing at these altitudes. A hand axe is often of service in cutting away obstructing boughs. I have seen sleeping apartments in a timberline clump of pines that have protected its occupants in a surprising degree of efficiency from wind and to some extent, rain and snow.

In the matter of location also in many regions of the west on account of the possibility of sudden freshets, one should avoid bivouacking in the bottoms of gullies and ravines. Those who have failed to take this precautionary advice, like the Irishman, "wake up dead." Whatever the location in the mountains, a careful choice of a spot, and ten or fifteen minutes in working it over usually pays big dividends in sleeping comfort which means conservation of what may be much needed energy.

CAUTIONS FOR CALIFORNIA MOUNTAINEERS

By many, mountaineering is regarded as a hazardous form of diversion. The occasional accidents — even fatalities, which from time to time occur — particularly in the Alps, seem to be responsible for this widespread impression. When we consider the extremely small number of such mishaps, the percentage of them is relatively small as to be almost negligible. The distressing part of the matter is that whether in the Alps or in the Sierra, a large portion of them are preventable, being due to either unwarranted chances being taken by novices or by the casual negligence of the expert. By far, the greater proportion have been the result of the former. People hang by a thread on a concealed crevasse, indulge in a dangerous glissade or attempt a rock climb beyond their skill.

The mountaineering in California is almost confined to the Sierra Nevada and to Mt. Shasta. In both, perceptible accidents have occurred. At the outset, one might state that "hiking in the mountains" and mountaineering are not synonymous expressions. So long as one does not leave the trails — the wide canyons, broad ridges and spacious upper basins characteristic of high mountains, he is hiking — not mountaineering and very slight danger is incurred. When, however, he quits them in order to ascend steep rock-strewn slopes, to scale precipitous walls, to pick his way along ragged knife-edges or cut his way across crevassed glaciers or up icy couloirs, he is mountaineering and is undergoing some hazard, the amount of which depends very greatly upon the skill and care which he and his companions exercise.

Genuine mountaineering skill implies a thorough knowledge of mountains and expertness in the use of equipment used in scaling them. Years of training are required to become highly proficient in either difficult rock or ice work. In our Sierra, however,

Clyde giving a belay to climbers in "Thin Man's Alley"
on Milestone Mountain. (Photo by William Walker Dulley,
The Sierra Club Albums, The Bancroft Library)

during the summer, there is no great amount of snow and ice work, the larger percentage of mountains being rock climbs of which only a small portion are technically speaking, really difficult. Neither the equipment or the training necessary to climb them safely is so great as for example in the case of the Alps or Canadian Rockies. Unfortunately, it happens that lack of skill and of proper equipment sometimes makes the climbing of comparatively easy mountains more dangerous than that of really difficult ones where proper equipment and care are employed.

In the case of the former, footwear is the most important item. A good hiking shoe may not necessarily be a good mountaineering one nor is any type of shoe good for all forms of climbing. Ice and snow may demand one form; rough rocks another; smooth rocks a third. Generally speaking, however, one can meet any ordinary contingencies by possessing two types — one with nailed leather soles and another with rubber or rope soles. Those provided with Hungarian coneheads are perhaps adequate for almost any rock climbing in the Sierra, but the one who wishes to be really prepared for both difficult rock and ice work will do well to use the Swiss edge or Tricouni nails. The former are of malleable iron made in several sizes and fit around the margin of the sole. They adhere remarkably well to many small inequalities in a rock surface and are excellent for snow and ice. They have the disadvantage of wearing smooth and thus becoming less efficient on both ice and rock. This, however, can be counteracted by using Tricouni nails. The latter are flat, have three teeth and are of hard steel. By driving them in the inner portion of the sole, along the edges between the edge nails on both, one has a very desirable combination which will "stick" to almost anything except very hard, smooth rock surfaces.

For dry, polished rock, rubber-soled tennis shoes are the best. Any form of basket-ball shoe is good, although probably crepe-soled ones adhere best. Rubber soles, however, are poor on loose material and execrable on wet surfaces of snow or ice. With the two types of shore-nailed and rubber soles, one is adequately outfitted, so far as foot gear is concerned, for anything that may be encountered in the Sierra.

Another valuable portion of equipment is the rope. In more difficult ranges, it is indispensable. In the Sierra, the regular alpine rope may be little used and often an encumbrance. It is probably, however, the only method by which the more difficult mountains of the Sierra can be safely climbed by novices. It should be remembered, however, that all novices on one rope is worse than no rope at all; that only when one or more of the party is skilled in its use, is it a safeguard.

Although Sierra climbing parties may not wish to be encumbered with a regulation alpine rope there should always be a light strong one at least 30-feet in length in the party. It may render a rather dangerous passage perfectly safe. A good rope is a 1/4" U.S. Marine test rope which weighs only about two pounds to the hundred feet and has a tensile strength of some seven hundred pounds.

Another safeguard is the use of an alpenstock or ice axe. In mountains where snow and ice abound, one or the other is indispensable. In our northwest, there are usually at least two ice axes to a rope — two to ten climbers — the others being provided with alpenstocks. In the Alps and Canadian Rockies, an ice axe is more commonly used.

Although more efficient, it is more difficult to manipulate and may be a source of danger in the hands of a novice. In the summer, the ice axe is only necessary on a few of the mountains — notably in the Palisades — excellent snow and ice climbing can be had in which ice axe is essential. Occasionally, the same is true elsewhere in the Sierra.

If simple yet adequate equipment such as that indicated above were used in the Sierra and the climber possessed a reasonable degree of skill in its use and exercised proper care, accidents in the Sierra would be very infrequent. Climbers would also derive increased pleasure from the possession and skillful manipulation of such equipment.

Climber walking a ledge on Whorl Mountain, northern Yosemite
(Photo by Pete Yamagata)

On Mt. Shasta, the equipment should more nearly approximate that employed in the Northwest. It's ascent up the usual route of the south face is technically a rather simple matter — a long snow trudge from a short distance about 8,000' in the early summer to the summit (14,161 feet above sea level) a grind up volcanic rock for a large portion of the distance culminating in snow and ice in the higher elevations in late summer. One's boots should always be equipped with either Swiss or Tricouni edge nails or screw calks. The last one is usually most easily prepared.

One should also be provided with either an alpenstock or an ice axe as both an assistance and safeguard in climbing. It is well also to have along a light rope such as that described above. He can then attack the noblest of California mountains with security under any ordinary conditions that may be encountered.

Deep winding chimney.
Wonderful view in every direction but the
upper Kings and Kern were enveloped
by a dense thundercloud, which soon came
bearing down upon the peak.
Heavy snow pellets drove against us while
thunder and lightening played about us.   The
rocks soon wet and we were
covered with snow and a stream began
to course down the chimney.
Drenched and cold.

Journal entry
Ten Lakes

THUNDERSTORMS IN THE SIERRA NEVADA

In my climbs in the Sierra Nevada and elsewhere I have had but few close calls from thunderstorms, as, generally speaking, I have preferred to be on my way elsewhere as soon as I am aware that one is approaching.

I have, however, along with others, had rather "dramatic" but always scatheless — thanks to Providence — experiences in electric storms on Sierra peaks. One of these was on top of the Black Kaweah, the summit of which we reached as Will Colby and party were leaving it.

On account of the friability of the rock along the route usually followed, particularly in a couloir which forms a considerable portion of the latter, he requested us to allow them three-quarters of an hour to get to a safe distance down the mountain.

From the summit I noticed a dark cloud mass to the southwest. Within a half hour this was obviously bearing down upon the Black Kaweah. I therefore told my party that if we did not want to be caught in a storm that we should be on our way down the mountain at once.

Scarcely had we started when the cloud mass swept over the summit of the mountain, and we were enveloped in a heavy snowstorm. Presently there were blinding flashes of lightning and deafening crashes of thunder; the former being located in a very disconcerting proximity as it struck a pinnacle. I seem to remember a halo of sparks about my old army hat. This, however, was doubtless pure hallucination.

Slowly and carefully we made our way down the mountain. Almost miraculously none of the friable rock gave way, producing a rockslide. As we drew away from the base of the mountain, the cloud mass slowly broke away, revealing a white mass from base to summit. Almost anything could have happened on this descent, but fortunately, nothing did.

Another rather 'dramatic' episode was on the occasion of the first ascent of Thunderbolt Peak. While Jules Eichorn and Glen Dawson were ascending the summit monolith, looking southward from the crest of this North Palisade, I noticed a cloud mass — or rather echelonned masses of clouds — approaching our mountain.

Presently, the first cloud mass enveloped the mountain and snow began to fall heavily. Scarcely had Jules and Glen left the monolith, when there was a flash and a crack as the thunderbolt struck its summit. We rather appropriately therefore, on thought, christened the mountain, Thunderbolt Peak.

Wet snow fell almost in masses which thawed quickly and soon torrents of water began to cascade down the mountainside, sweeping along rocks which went crashing down. Again almost anything could have happened on this climb but fortunately, nothing did.

The above, of course, are very unusual experiences. Generally speaking, in the Sierra Nevada, the climber has sufficient warning of the approach of a storm to be a safe distance down the mountain when it actually strikes. It should be borne in mind, however, that the course followed by summer storm clouds in the Sierra is sometimes rather erratic. One, apparently headed directly toward the mountain, on which one happens to be, may suddenly swerve and strike elsewhere. On the contrary also, one apparently on the way to another mountain may suddenly swing around and come bearing down upon the peak which the climber happens to be occupying.

It should be remembered, that it is difficult to appraise an approaching storm cloud. An apparently threatening one may prove to be nothing worse than a snow or rain squall, while a deceivingly looking harmless one, into an extremely severe electric storm and the narrow top of a mountain is just about the worst place to experience such a phenomenon.

HIGH SIERRA AVALANCHES

Avalanches are much more numerous in the High Sierra during the winter and spring than those who have not spent considerable time there are aware. Their number varies greatly being much more frequent and of greater volume during seasons of high precipitation. That comparatively slight damage has been done to property and few lives lost is due in large measure to the fact that most occur where there is little property to destroy and no person in the pathway.

With the annual increase of visitors to the Sierra for skiing and climbing, the hazard to life and limb is enhanced, particularly to those who do not know when or where slides may occur. Those who do may not come to grief in a single season.

Snowslides in the higher portions of the mountains take place most frequently in couloirs or chutes. After heavy snowfalls numerous slides course down. They are most likely in winter or within the day following a storm. In spring, after a storm, almost as soon as the sunshine strikes new snow, it may let go and come rushing down the couloir. After a storm in May, I have seen as many as a dozen slides coursing down as many couloirs in beautiful snowfalls.

Avalanches take place on smooth slopes on steep mountain faces. Powder snow does not cling to these faces. If it happens to

Norman Clyde Peak (Photo by Pete Yamagata)

be wet, as sometimes happens, even in the high Sierra, a considerable amount may adhere to the rocks. As the temperature warms this usually sloughs off in avalanches.

During winters of heavy snowfall, slides may occur in unexpected places. They may even come down rough south-facing slopes where slides seldom or never take place during winters of normal snowfall. Snowslides may sweep all the snow down to the underlying rocks, perhaps taking along the rocks. Then the avalanche gives a crashing sound as it goes plunging down. If composed almost entirely of snow, it may only give a hissing sound, audible for no great distance. If of powder snow and the volume is great, a cloud of flying snow will be carried high into the air.

Many slides do not reach the underlying terrain. Except on protected slopes or basins, snow that falls in the Sierra may be packed by the wind or thaw on the surface. As the temperature drops, a crust is formed. If alternate thawing and freezing continues, nevé, or granular snow is formed. By spring, much of the snow, particularly on exposed slopes, is of this form.

Rough slopes which would prevent snow from sliding are sometimes smoothed over. Should a heavy snow fall on such a surface, particularly if the slope is above forty-five degrees, the danger of a slide is great. Many of the spring slides are of this type. Often these are not dangerous unless one happens to be in a confined space, such as a couloir, or if they happen to be a sheet-slide so wide that one cannot get beyond their margin.

Slides in the Sierra are likely to be narrow. After a storm, I have seen numerous ones of new snow come down, each making a peculiar hissing sound. I have skied across the path of one and, wheeling, watched the slide sweep with its peculiar sliding, rolling motion. Avalanches usually start slowly. A crack runs along, then slowly widens and a sheet of snow begins to move. Once started, the acceleration may be great. If it travels three-thousand feet down a steep slope, it may reach express-train speed. Its momentum being significant, it may run across several hundred yards of terrain at the foot. If the slide results from a collapsing cornice, it may however, simply go plunging down the mountainside.

Generally, there is little danger to one who knows when and where snowslides may occur. In many years of rambling about at high elevations, only on two occasions did I incur any such danger. Once, after climbing through a notch in the upper rim of a cliff and entering a couloir, I stepped to one side. As I did so, I heard a swishing sound, and an avalanche swept down the notch through which I had just climbed.

On another occasion, weary of slogging through wet snow well up to my knees, I hit upon the idea of starting miniature snowslides and riding them. This I did by sitting down heavily, causing the layer of new snow to begin to slide. The acceleration was rapid. Eventually I struck a shadowed area, where an icy crust had formed. Instantly, the slide shot forward, with a cliff only a short distance ahead. By swimming and rolling, I managed to get off the slide and watched it vanish over the cliff. That was the last time that I deliberately rode a snowslide.

A Tragedy in the Sierra Nevada

I have led scores of parties, hundred of people up mountains of the Sierra Nevada and other high ranges of the west without any person incurring anything worse than slight injuries and very few of these. Yet on one occasion, I went out on what was intended primarily to be a skiing trip with another man and returned alone. I returned alone, despite the fact that I have repeatedly risked my life for the sake of others both alive and dead.

William Dulley, the man by whom I was accompanied, was apparently an excellent outdoorsman. He had climbed a considerable number of peaks in California during which he had been involved with several rather strenuous and prolonged adventures. He had also engaged in some mountaineering in the Rocky Mountains of Canada and had done considerable exploring, chiefly in the form of boating and snowshoeing in the Canadian Northwest.

Although he had been with me a considerable portion of two winters at my cabin in the Sierra Nevada, I had gone with him on very few trips. This was in part because I was occupied with other interests in part from the fact that in spite of an apparently excellent record, I had not entire confidence in William Dulley. When venturing on a winter trip of any consequence in the Sierra Nevada, one never knows for certain whether weather conditions may not be encountered which with may demand the utmost stamina and perseverance to survive. Somehow I doubted whether William had this necessary stamina.

He had, it is true, stood the test of several rather strenuous and hazardous experiences in the mountains, but he was always slow — to me painfully so. His unwarranted deliberations led me to suspect that possibly his heart might not be altogether what it

(Photographer, unknown, Wynne Benti Collection)

should be. Yet, I had never seen any indications of undue palpitation of his heart which are reasonably obvious at high altitude in this part of those suffering from any defect in this organ. This may, however, have been because he was always so very deliberate in his movements. He never displayed any superfluous energy.

Incidentally also he was somewhat of an enigma to me. To being extremely non-committal, he added a habit of occasional dissimilation and equivorism. Slight as this was, it seemed to indicate to me that consciously or unconsciously, something was being concealed. His mental reaction always appeared to be very slow. William Dulley, therefore was not a man who had my unquestioned confidence as being a man capable of meeting an unusual emergency, especially a case of "smash thought or perish."

Winter had apparently passed, and William was planning to return to Los Angeles in the near future. Knowing that he wished to visit Piute Pass, on the crest of the Sierra Nevada, 11,409 feet in elevation above the sea, and had failed to do so on several solitary attempts, I thought that he might welcome my going with him over the pass. Skiing in the undulating above-timberline basin beyond the pass should be excellent, and the weather conditions being favorable, there might be an opportunity of making an ascent of Mount Humphreys, a formidable peak 13,986 feet in elevation.

During the first week of April, there had been a succession of light storms. On the morning of the 6th however, the north wind in the Sierra Nevada, usually an indication of clearing weather, was blowing the few remaining clouds southward. The forecast of the weather bureau was also to the same effect. Even so I thought that it might be advisable to wait another day or so, but as William was soon to leave, I decided that the venture would be at least reasonably safe.

We therefore motored a few miles to the end of the road, an elevation of some 9,000 feet, and then continued up the canyon on skis. As we neared timberline, a storm from the southwest came swooping over the crest of the Sierra. Falling snow presently convinced us that any attempt to scale Mount Humphreys might be foolhardy. A few inches or even a foot of snow would in all likelihood improve skiing conditions in the basin beyond the pass. Being April also, it did not seem likely that this approaching storm would be one of any great length or severity. We therefore decided to continue across the pass.

Having reached it unhurt, we headed southwestward down a rather gradual slope, in search of at least a tolerably suitable camping place. After going perhaps a mile involving a descent of some five hundred feet we came to a large rock with a cavity in the snow, there about six feet deep, which seemed to offer some shelter. Nearby was a knoll on which stood a number of dead pines. We therefore threw down our packs, but not being altogether satisfied we explored about a half mile farther, without however, finding anything better.

Upon examining the cavity upon our return, I was still less satisfied. It had evidently been caused by the wind eddying about the rock. Should the storm prove a serious one, the wind might sweep through it in an uncomfortable fashion and coming from a certain direction might even fill it with flying snow. Realizing this, I suggested to William that it might be well to continue to a clump of pine trees a matter of a mile or thereabouts to the north. He replied that there was no wood there. This remark puzzled me both because I knew he had never been there, and the fact that I could plainly see a number of dead upright pines which could readily be cut down with the axe which I was carrying. Being that it was getting late however, we decided to make camp in this cavity.

After cutting and carrying a considerable supply of wood, we made a rather large fire. The heat being reflected from the bank of snow to the rock and back, this camp soon became fairly comfortable. The snow continued falling during the entire night and with some interruptions during the following day, in which we did little but getting some more wood and cook some food, construct pine bough beds, and attempt to dry some socks and gloves — a futile attempt however, as the falling snow wet them as fast as the fire dried them.

During the record night the storm increased in severity. The snow fell more heavily and continuously and the wind blew with increased velocity. The snow drifted over me in such a fashion as I lay in the lee of a bank, that I was obliged to roll several feet in order to avoid being completely covered by it. When day broke the storm appeared to increase in severity.

The first words from William were, "let's break camp." To this I did not respond very favorably, because I was comfortably snug in my snowy covering and because I was averse to moving in such weather conditions. During the next hour, however, the "break camp" suggestion was repeated a wearisome number of times.

I thought over this matter, per and err. I knew that William was uncomfortable from the fact that the snow, having been blown in under the heavy canvas "tarp", not sewn into a bag, had to some extent been melted by heat from his body and had soaked through his down sleeping bag which was not water-proof. There would also be some risk of being caught in a snowslide at one point, but aside from that, it seemed to me that if I broke a way for him, through the ten feet or more of new loose snow that he should be able to reach the end of the road on the other side of the crest. I therefore decided to return.

After crawling out of my sleeping bag, I began to reach about for my ski boots — which should have been thrust down into my sleeping bag, buried somewhere beneath several feet of snow. I soon found them but the socks which I was wearing were filled with snow and the reserve ones were in no better condition.

In about a half hour our packs were made up. My skis were standing upright in the snow with a pair of canvas socks — for climbing purposes attached to them. William's seal skins were hanging in the rock. Their buckles being frozen, after some little attempt to put them on his skis, he rolled them up and thrust them into his pack.

Finding one's way upward through the new fallen snow was

heavy and exhausting work. With his waxed skis, William could not ascend at as steep an angle as I, even though I decreased the angle of ascent on a disagreeably frequent basis on his behalf. Furthermore, my socks being moist from melted snow, I knew that I could not do so without running the risk of freezing my feet. Neither were my hands adequately protected and my jacket was so frozen that it could not be put on. I was therefore in my shirt sleeves in a driving wind, waiting it seemed for infinity for a man who came blundering along with the best climbing device available for skis — in his pack.

William also indulged in some "back seat" driving by repeatedly suggesting that we were too far to the right, although no land marks were visible, the surrounding peaks being completely shrouded in storm clouds. In response to the reiterations, I veered somewhat to the right and as a result, I suddenly realized that we had gone at least far enough to be on this pass — but were not. Removing our packs and sitting down on a rock, we considered matters, both coming to the conclusion that the pass was slightly behind and some distance to the north.

Swinging northward, however, we gained the possibility of being caught at one point in a snowslide, the hazards of the trip appearing to have passed. There being too much loose snow for good skiing on the way down, I decided not to remove the canvas socks from my skis, and thus probably avoid several falls which would be disagreeable and possibly dangerous on account of the rather heavy weight of my pack.

The wind in the narrow pass being unpleasantly cold and thinking that William would be on my heels, I crossed it without panic and began the descent of the east slope. In about a quarter of a mile, I came to the brink of a steep dip of about a hundred feet. Knowing that the mantle of new snow would slide if I put my weight on it, I paused. Upon looking back, William was nowhere in sight.

As I swung sidewise to the drop, my skis cut the new snow at its rim in such a fashion, that a strip, perhaps twenty feet in width broke away and slid to the bottom. I then slithered down sidewise on the old firm snow exposed by the slide.

I then skied about fifty yards to one side and waited for William, as I was afraid that should he be able to get up any speed on his waxed skis, that he might go plunging over the drop. By and by, he came along at his usual gait. I called to him advising him to come over to the bluff where I did. He got on the bluff safely and advanced toward me. As he approached I scrutinized him carefully, but could see no indication of there being anything wrong. I did not ask him why he had delayed.

We then pushed steadily along with our occasional pause, and, except for the unevenness of the snow, progress for some distance was only moderately difficult. In a mile or thereabouts, I reached a lake. Upon looking back, however, somewhat to my surprise, William was again nowhere in sight. In my shirt sleeves and with wet feet, I sat down on a rock, with a cold wind blowing and waited. By and by he came along and he came ahead of me, remarked that he had gone aside to look for ski runs and had a couple of falls. Such tactics on such a day to me were nothing less than amazing. I was furiously angry, but perhaps unfortunately said nothing, thinking that it could not possibly occur again.

In another half mile, we were nearing another lake. We began to go down over the brow of the bluffs. The snow suddenly became extremely powdery and fluffy like heaps of down in which one sank down. Realizing at a glance that everywhere along the bluffs, this was the condition of the snow, it was merely a case of plowing through it to the lake, then only several hundred feet distant.

When about halfway down I observed that William had abandoned the trail made for him, the Lord only knows why — and was making one of his own. Thinking however that he would make the lake a few minutes after me, I continued forcing my way through the snow.

On the lake, the skiing was good as much as the snow had been blown off it. Supposing that William, with his waxed skis,

An example of Clyde's handwritten manuscripts (Wynne Benti Collection) would soon overtake me, I went along steadily. Suddenly, so quickly in fact that I did not have time to turn around, the wind doubled in velocity and the atmosphere suddenly became filled with a driving mass of powdery snow. I could see but a few yards and the wind made such an uproar in the cliffs above, that a voice could be heard only a very short distance. So violent was the gale that I frequently could remain upright only by propping myself with my ski poles.

Where William was I did not know as he had left the trail made for him. He was not far but in a furious mountain blizzard, a few rods may be a long distance. It was probably impossible to face it and even should I succeed in advancing against, the man for whom I was searching in the whirling volume of snow might slip past me unnoticed. I therefore did the only thing which seemed feasible — proceeded at half speed calling out at frequent intervals.

At the lower end of the lake, a matter of perhaps a half mile, I paused for a short while. The wind was so violent that I could remain standing only by propping myself. Immediately below the lake was a rather steep incline terminating in a line of cliffs several hundred feet high. With two feet or more of new snow on this slope, I saw that it was in a hazardous condition. Realizing that it might require some time to find a way across it — if indeed I should succeed in getting across it at all — I thought it best to go on. Meanwhile, I thought, William would probably come up and find a way ready for him.

I had not proceeded far when I observed a slide had already come over the bluffs immediately above. A mass of snow of some volume suddenly struck the snow a short distance ahead of me. Presently, I noticed a crack in the snow moving along ahead of me. Every mountain climber knows that this means "get off and get off quickly." I therefore swung my skis around and retraced my skis across the slope. By carefully surveying it however, I picked a course along which at no point would one be far from a line. In the event of a slide, by a quick run I might be able to grab a tree before the snow should gain any great speed.

Somewhat to my surprise, I succeeded in crossing the dangerous incline without starting a slide. As I looked back and upward, William was not to be seen along the snow. In my shirt sleeves and with wet feet, I was already half-frozen by numerous waitings. In return for all my efforts, he had made blunder after blunder and had not even consistently followed a trail made for him. My patience was exhausted. If he was having trouble, if not entirely spent, he could throw away his pack and follow me, unburdened and with a way made for him, he should soon be able to overtake me. If spent, he should crawl into his sleeping bag and there await my return on the following morning. Mountaineers have done so numbers of times and have survived — even been reasonably comfortable.

I therefore continued down over a long, open slope, not however without pausing frequently and looking back. Below the line of cliffs which I had passed, the wind was much less violent and the air was comparatively free from flying snow. The temperature was, however, rapidly dropping. Beyond the open slope I passed through a rather broken strip of terrain covered with timber. Past this, I continued along a mile or so of open canyon floor and then along a snow-covered road around a point and down to the portion of the road which had already been opened.

There, at seven o'clock, I knocked at the door of a cabin occupied by a miner. In the lighted and heated room I presently discovered that the ends of my fingers and toes were frozen — an hour more and they would probably have been entirely so. Several hours were spent in thawing out my frozen members and filling myself with hot food.

Knowing his usual rear guard habits however, I still had some expectations of William arriving. No one, however, having appeared by ten o'clock, I retired in a neighboring cabin.

Awakening on the following morning, later than I had expected, I discovered that the miner had already gone to work. There was no wood in the cabin which I was occupying and my fingers were by this time in such a condition that I could not very well dig any out of a snow-covered heap of it out of doors. I therefore got on my skis and went a half mile to another cabin at which I got breakfast and returned.

The storm had passed over during the night. The sky was now blue and without a cloud and the sun shone bright from over a mountain. I thawed out my pack sufficiently to get out some food. Taking it and an axe, I returned up the canyon. Although my tracks alone were coming down it, I still had hopes that William was either alive in his sleeping bag or was on his way down.

Proceeding slowly and carefully up the canyon, especially through the stretch of forest, I observed and hollered at intervals. I eventually neared the line of cliffs without discovering anything. Thinking that he might have been carried over the latter, I scrutinized them closely with a pair of binoculars. Nothing, however, was to be seen.

The snow on the crestline having been packed firm during the night of this wind, I made the traverse without difficulty or danger. As I was looking about, a short distance above the bluffs, a prostrate form half buried in snow attracted my attention. The portion of the remains indicated a sudden collapse. William had stuck his ski poles in the snow, removed his pack and dropped dead. His autopsy later revealed the fact that his heart had actually "popped." My surmises as to him both physically and mentally were, unfortunately only too true.

View of the wonderful cloud effects above the high Sierra from the ridge above the lakes. Abundant snow among the trees, chiefly hemlock and mountain pines about the lakes. All the lakes partially or wholly frozen, except one. Wonderful reflection of the forest and snow-covered mountains in the second lake. Stillness, solitude, and seclusion of the place.

Journal entry

Ten Lakes

FINALE
by Thomas H. Jukes

Norman Clyde died in Big Pine, California in December 1972 at the age of 87. He had lived as every alpinist wants to live, but as none of them dare to do, and so he had a unique life. When he died, I felt that an endangered species had become extinct. For half a century, he had spent spring, summer and fall in the Sierra Nevada, and his winters on its magnificent eastern flanks, usually as the caretaker of some mountain lodge, empty until next season, alone in the untrodden snow. His ascents, nearly all in the Sierra, must have numbered in the thousands.

Climbers today tote horrible little mechanical stoves with blue cylinders of low-molecular-weight hydrocarbons prepared by the petroleum industry on which to warm their pre-cooked freeze-dried shrimp creole. Norman carried a cast-iron frying pan and some chunks of dead wood in his gigantic old knapsack to cook fresh trout. He was large, solitary, taciturn and irritable — like the North Palisade in a thunderstorm, and he could also be mellow and friendly, like the afternoon sun on Evolution Lake. It is impossible to think of Norman Clyde without remembering the glories of the southern High Sierra, because you were always liable to meet him up there if you wandered far enough. He was a reader of the classics, and carried books with him. He was famous for mountain rescues. His last camp was at 10,000 feet in the Fourth Recess of Mono Creek and he had to cross the main crest of the Sierra Nevada to get to it, at the age of 85. He was the only man I have known who gave himself up completely to a passionate love of the mountains. In return, the mountains spared him a hundred times as he clambered alone to their summits by many a new route. And, they let him die of old age, in full view of their peaks.

CLYDE'S FIRST ASCENTS IN THE SIERRA NEVADA*

Electra Peak (12,442')	1914	CG
Parker Peak (12,851')	1914	CG
Mt. Huxley (13,086')	8-20	CG
Dragon Peak (12,995')	1920	CG
Triple Divide Peak (11,607')	1920	CG
Peak 12,415'	7-22	CG
Peak 11,920'+ **	8-9-22	CG
Diamond Peak (13,126')	8-22	CG
Mt. Lippencott (12,260')	1922	CG
Mt. McAdie – North Peak. (13,680')	1922	CG
Gray Kaweah (13,680')	1922	MR
Mt. Irvine (13,770')	6-25	CG
Mt. Le Conte (13,960')	6-25	CG
Mt. Mallory (13,850')	6-25	CG
North Guard (13,327')	7-12-25	CG
Mt. Genevra (13,055')	7-15-25	CG
Mt. Jordan (13,344')	7-15-25	CG
The Hermit (12,360')	8-2-25	SCB
Emerald Peak (12,543')	8-8-25	CG
Peak 11,778'	8-8-25	CG
Agassiz Needle/Mt. Agassiz(13,891')	8-30-25	CG
Giraud Peak (12,608')	9-1-25	CG
Peak 12,861'	11-22-25	CG
Mt. Carillon (13,552')	1925	CG
Mt. Lamarck (13,417')	1925	CG
Lone Pine Peak (12,944')	1925	CG
Kearsarge Peak (12,598')	1925	CG
Peak 12,000'+	1925	CG
Peak 12,400'+	1925	MR
Peak 12,720'+	1925	CG
Peak 13,040'	1925	CG
Peak 13,231'	1925	CG
Peak 13,360'	1925	CG
Peak 13,320'	4-4-26	CG

Candlelight Peak (12,000'+)	6-26	SCB
Peak 13,840'+	6-22-26	CG
Mt. Russell (14,086')	6-24-26	CG
Trojan Peak (13,950')	6-26-26	CG
Point 13,920'+	6-27-26	CG
Mt. Emerson (13,204')	7-3-26	CG
Mt. Goethe (13,264')	7-5-26	SCB
Peak 13,112'	7-7-26	SCB
West Spur Peak (12,640')	9-19-26	CG
Peak 12,225'	9-19-26	CG
Independence Peak (11,744')	1926	SCB
Lookout Point (10,144')	1926	CG
Mt. Gayley (13,510')	6-10-27	CG
Inconsolable Range/Cloudripper (13,525')	6-15-27	CG
Deerhorn Mtn. (13,265')	7-8-27	CG
Piute Crags – No.5 (12,480+)	1927	CG
Table Mtn. (13,630')	7-26-27	CG
Peak 12,866'	1927	CG
Mt. McAdie – Middle Peak (13,680+)	6-28	CG
Mt. Morrison (12,268')	6-22-28	CG
Clyde Minaret (12,281')	6-27-28	CG
Mt. Baldwin (12,614')	7-2-28	SCB
Bloody Mtn (12,544')	7-3-28	CG
Mt. Gilbert (13,103')	9-15-28	CG
Mt. Robinson (12,967')	7-6-29	MR
Peak 13,917'	6-9-30	CG
Peak 13,520'+	6-14-30	CG
Peak 12,840'+	7-4-30	CG
North Palisade – NW Pk./Starlight (14,080')	7-9-30	CG
Basin Mtn – W Pk (13,240')	11-8-30	SCB
Basin Mtn – E Pk (12,880+)	11-9-30	SCB
Peak 13,120'+	6-27-31	CG
Peak 13,090'	7-5-31	CG
Peak 13,355'	7-16-31	SCB
Echo Peaks, No. 3 (11,160'+)	7-31-31	SCB
Thunderbolt Pk. (14,003')	8-13-31	CG
Peak 13,323'	9-6-31	CG
Peak 12,571'	9-29-31	CG
Peak 12,993'	11-7-31	SCB
Four Gables (12,720')	1931	CG

Slide Mtn.(11,084')	1931	CG
Pinnacle Ridge (13,040')	4-4-32	NC
Peak 12,640'	5-26-32	NC
Peak 12,893'	7-17-32	CG
Mt. Stewart (12,200')	8-14-32	CG
Mt. Hutchings (10,785')	1933	CG
Clyde Spires – N Pk (13,240')	7-22-33	CG
Clyde Spires – S Pk (12,960+)	7-22-33	CG
Kehrlein Minaret (11,611')	8-23-33	CG
Wotan's Throne (12,726')	1933	CG
Devil's Crag #10 (11,950')	6-23-34	CG
Devil's Crag #11 (11,950')	6-23-34	CG
Devil's Crag # 3 (12,350')	6-24-34	CG
Devil's Crag # 4 (12,250')	6-24-34	CG
Devil's Crag # 5 (12,250')	6-25-34	CG
Devil's Crag # 6 (12,250')	6-25-34	CG
Devil's Crag # 7 (12,250')	6-25-34	CG
Devil's Crag # 8 (11,250')	6-25-34	CG
Mt. Morgan (12,999')	7-9-34	CG
Mt. Huntington (12,405')	7-14-34	CG
Peak 12,318'	7-14-34	CG
Peak 12,408'	7-16-34	MR
Mt. Hopkins (12,304')	7-16-34	CG
Peak 12,880'+	7-18-34	CG
Peak 12,691'	7-18-34	CG
Mono Rock (11,554')	7-18-34	CG
Peak 12,804'	July 1935	CG
Peak 12,852'	July 1935	CG
Peak 13,163'	July 1935	CG
Peak 12,372'	8-25-35	CG
Peak 12,400'+	9-4-35	CG
Peak 13,045'	9-14-35	CG
Peak 11,844'	9-16-35	CG
Peak 11,719	9-16-35	CG
Peak 12,916	6-13-36	NC
Inconsolable Range (13,278')	6-15-37	CG
Mt. Izaak Walton (12,077')	7-20-38	NC
Peak 12,563	1938	CG
Goodale Mtn. (12,769')	7-23-39	CG
Kid Mtn./Kid Pk.(11,458')	7-2-40	CG

Cardinal Mtn. (13,392')	'20s	SCB
Mt. Johnson (12,871')	before 1939	CG
Thor Pk. (12,303')	before 1936	CG

*This list does not include all of Norman Clyde's first route ascents in the Sierra Nevada, only his first ascents of peaks. His first route ascents number in the hundreds. Most recent peak elevations have been used when available. Clyde's references to elevations throughout the text of "Close Ups of the High Sierra" were the current ones in use at the time.

CG = A Climber's Guide to the High Sierra, 1954
MR = Mountain Records of the Sierra Nevada, 1937
NC = Journals of Norman Clyde, unpublished.
SCB = Sierra Club Bulletin
**11,920+ = elevation of highest contour line.

SELECTED WRITINGS OF NORMAN CLYDE
with Bibliographical References

Touring Topics

June 1927	A May Day Ascent of Mt. Whitney
July 1927	Mountaineering in the Sierra Nevada
August 1927	Scaling Mt. Humphreys
November 1927	The Ascent of Mt. Darwin
March 1928	The First Ascent of Mt. Mallory and Mt. Irvine
April-July 1928	"Close Ups" of Our High Sierra
November 1928	To the Summit
March 1929	On Snowshoes in the Sierra
July 1929	Climbing Glacier's Highest Peak
September 1929	An Ascent of the Grand Teton
October 1929	Mountaineering in the Canadian Rockies
August 1930	Canyons of the Southern Sierras
November 1930	High-Low
May 1931	Along the Sierran Crestline
August 1931	Up the Middle Palisade
December 1931	Up the East Face of Whitney
April 1932	Over the Crests of Southland Urban Mountains
September 1932	The Conquest of Lower California's Highest Peak
July 1932	Over the Sierra from Sequoia to Whitney

Westways

May 1934	Death on a Mountain Top
January 1935	Wintering on Yosemite's Crag
September 1935	Glaciers of the Sierra Nevada
April 1936	Up Mt. Shasta from the East
June 1937	Mountain Sheep of the Sierra
September 1938	Ramble on Sierran Trails
November 1938	Climbing El Picacho del Diablo
February 1940	Skiing to Winter Summits
February 1941	Holing Up for a Sierran Winter
June 1941	Above the Timber Line
July 1941	Up Bear Creek Spire in a Summer Storm
January 1942	Weather-wise Buck